RELATIONAL DISCIPLESHIP

Transformed by God's Love

*And we all, with unveiled face, beholding
as in a mirror the glory of the Lord, are being
transformed into the same image from glory to glory,
just as from the Lord, the Spirit (2 Corinthians 3:18).*

David Ferguson

Relationship Press

Relationship Press • P.O. Box 201808 • Austin, TX 78720-1808
Phone: 1-800-881-8008 • Fax: 1-512-795-0853

ISBN–1-893307-50-6

Table of Contents

Acknowledgements

"I pray that the eyes of your heart may be enlightened, so that you will know . . . what are the riches of the glory of His inheritance in the saints" (Ephesians 1:18 NASB).

In the shaping of this resource, I have been abundantly blessed by God's glorious riches "in the saints." His encouragement and affirmation come often through the denominational leaders, ministers, and pastors we serve through the Great Commandment Network. In particular, Pastors Roger and Julie Barrier with Casas Adobes Church in Tucson, and Pastor Alister and Christine Mort in the U.K., share the Lord's support as they co-labor with us in seeking to hear and shape His fresh Great Commandment message.

Larry Duncan and the Center for Biblical Leadership team provided valuable reflection and reaction during the field-test phase of this course. Leonard Albert and Ray Hughes with Church of God Lay Ministries also partnered with us, providing the vision and resources to help make this course a reality.

John Duncan provided invaluable coordination and editing related to all of the *Relational Discipleship* materials, while the staff of the White Wing Publishing House, including Joann Nope, Perry Horner, Virginia Chatham, Elizabeth Witt, and Diann Stewart lent their expertise in the areas of layout, art direction, proofreading, and printing.

Dr. Dennis Lindsay and Dr. Jack Hatcher with Christ for the Nations in Dallas, Texas, cooperated in providing a "laboratory" audience from the around the world for the supportive media material. Mike Frazier displayed his usual creative genius in coordinating the development of the multimedia components of this course. Ron Proctor and the Campus Crusade Life Builders national leadership team also participated in the video development process, as well as giving encouragement concerning the value of the *Relational Discipleship* message.

God's supportive riches were also provided through the work of the Intimate Life team, including Jan Dodd, Katie Ferguson, Kim Friesz, and Courtney Hartman. Terri Snead, my oldest daughter and a member of the ILM team, always accompanies me on these curriculum "journeys," seeking as best she can to clarify my sometimes scattered impressions and reflections.

Finally, I would like to extend deep gratitude to Jim Walter, ILM's Team Leader for Training and Resource Development, who provided support in the development of this message, assisted with the structure of the course, coordinated the field tests, and developed the Facilitator's Guide. God worked through Jim in all of these ways so that I would not be alone.

David

Preface

"Men of Issachar . . . understood the times and knew what Israel should do" (1 Chronicles 12:32).

In order to "understand the times" in which we live, we must address the issue of relevance. Is the church having a relevant, significant impact on our world today? Are the saints truly being conformed into the image of Christ? Is church ministry really about events, activities, and keeping up with the latest popular curricula and programs? Are we truly fulfilling Christ's Great Commission to make disciples (Matthew 28:19, 20)?

Restoring relevance to the body of Christ requires that we carefully consider how we relate to God's Son, God's Word, and God's people.

- Do we truly experience intimacy with Christ?

- Have we moved beyond merely seeking to believe and obey the Bible, and begun to experience a loving relationship with the God who wrote it?

- Do we honestly walk in vulnerable, accountable fellowship with a few other saints?

- Can we relate to those who do not know Christ? Are we truly "friends of sinners," sharing with them not only the Gospel, but our very lives?

- In our churches and ministry settings, do we see others becoming true disciples by experiencing intimacy with God's Son, encountering God at the point of His Word, and participating in the divine mystery of true fellowship?

The first century church turned the world upside down for Jesus by embracing these relational principles. If we are to survive in our own unique cultural and historical context, we must do the same. This resource is our invitation to you to join us in a movement of restoring relevance to Christ's church through the transforming power of His love!

Dr. David Ferguson

Welcome to *Relational Discipleship!*

Relational Discipleship is a course of study designed to help you discover God's purpose and calling for your life and to encourage you to pursue the lifelong, life-changing process of becoming like Jesus.

This *Relational Discipleship* workbook is intended to serve as the participants' guide for the course. It includes everything participants need to thoroughly experience the *Relational Discipleship* resource.

This workbook includes the following features:

- **Key *Relational Discipleship* Principles**—These are introduced as text boxes in each chapter. These foundational principles are then discussed in the text of the workbook.
- **Experiences With God's Word**—Each chapter includes an opportunity to truly experience God's Word together. At these times, participants will have the opportunity to become "doers of the Word" (James 1:22 KJV).
- **Experiences With God's People**—Each chapter includes an opportunity for you to allow the Lord to work through His people. As true fellowship is experienced, you will be empowered to reflect His character and to demonstrate His care and compassion for each other.
- **Experiences With God's Son**—Each chapter also includes at least one opportunity for participants to pause and reflect on God's Son. Through these times of quiet reflection and meditation, a deeper love for Christ will be born.
- **Follow-Up Projects**—At the end of each of the first seven chapters are follow-up projects that present further opportunities for spiritual growth. Participants will be challenged to consider practical life application of *Relational Discipleship* principles, engage in Bible studies, develop specific ministry skills, practice spiritual disciplines, and memorize scriptures. These things will help to continue the Spirit's work of exercising ourselves toward godliness (1 Timothy 4:7).

EXPERIENCING THIS COURSE IN COMMUNITY

We were never intended to live the Christian life alone. Like the early church, we are to be devoted to real fellowship, or *koinonia*—open, honest, authentic relationships with other people. Thus, this course is not intended to be a study that you undertake alone. Rather, you are to be coached or mentored by another person who has already completed the course and is continuing to practice its principles.

Spiritual formation is intended to be lived out in community, and it is to be multiplied: "The things you have heard me say . . . entrust to reliable men who will also be qualified to teach others" (2 Timothy 2:2). "Teach the older women. . . . Then they can train the younger women . . ." (Titus 2:3, 4). If at all possible, seek out someone with whom you can experience *Relational Discipleship*. You might also wish to work through this course with a small group or class.

Whether you experience *Relational Discipleship* one-to-one or in a small group, we trust that your journey through this course will not be just another study, but rather will radically change your life and ministry!

HOW TO GET THE MOST OUT OF THIS RESOURCE

In order to get the most benefit and blessing from this resource, we urge you to do the following:

1. **Set aside time each week to read the chapter and work through the Experiential Exercises.** This will prepare you for your interactions with a partner or small group and enrich your personal understanding of each chapter.

2. **If you are working through this resource with a friend or ministry partner, we urge you to make time each week to work through and discuss the exercises.** Make your meetings a priority in your schedule, and come prepared to interact appropriately.

3. **If you are working through this resource with a small group, we urge you to make it a priority to attend each small group session.** Make your meetings a consistent part of your schedule, and come prepared to interact appropriately. You may also want to make notes and then reflect on the responses of fellow group members from each meeting. We urge you to get to know each person in your group in a meaningful way, show interest in their lives, and demonstrate supportive care.

4. **The following "Participant Promise" page presents some ways in which you can make the most of your experience with this workbook.** We suggest that you read it over and carefully discuss it with your partner or group before making this commitment.

PARTICIPANT PROMISE

We invite each participant to commit to the following in order to enhance their personal and communal experience of this resource:

I will spend time between sessions completing the chapters with honesty and sincerity.

I will be open and willing for God to show me how I can better follow Him as He is formed in me.

I will participate in learning sessions fully, openly, and honestly.

I will seek to give care as others may need it, and receive care as I may need it.

I will be willing to receive feedback from those who know me in my group, team, or family so that I might experience the growth and change that God intends for me through this course.

_____   Date
Name

Introduction:
The Mystery of Our Calling

"The disciples came to him and asked, 'Why do you speak to the people in parables?' He replied, 'The knowledge of the secrets of the kingdom of heaven has been given to you, but not to them'" (Matthew 13:10, 11).

There are many secrets and mysteries of the kingdom of God that Jesus has revealed to those who follow Him. This course is about one such mystery: our divine calling as citizens of God's kingdom to be transformed into His image (2 Corinthians 3:18).

Everything in creation has been given a calling by God. The sun and planets themselves have been placed in such a way as to provide for the sustenance of life. If the sun was closer to the earth than it is, or farther from it, most of our planet would be uninhabitable. Nature continually maintains the precarious equilibrium that is necessary for our survival. Every part of the ecological system has an important place, a purpose to fulfill—a calling.

The same is true for you and me. We each have a divine calling. When we receive Jesus Christ as our Savior, trusting that He paid for our sin when He died on the Cross of Calvary, His Spirit comes to dwell within us, revealing and empowering the calling that God has placed on our lives—not just a general calling, but also a personal one. The question is not just "Why did God create humanity?" but also "Why are **you** here on this planet?"

Perhaps it is already clear to us that part of our calling, like that of the 12 disciples, is to be followers of Jesus. Scripture also tells us that we are called not only to follow Christ, but to become like Him (Romans 8:29). A common label for this process by which God makes us more and more like Jesus is "spiritual formation." But what does that really mean? How can we live out genuine discipleship in today's increasingly challenging world?

Tragically, it seems as though few of us have an answer to this question. How else can we explain the fact that the church (particularly in the western world) looks so much more like the surrounding culture than it looks like Jesus? Churches conduct an enormous number of events—seminars, workshops, conferences, concerts, retreats, conventions, and more. If events could produce Christlike character, we would be the most mature followers of Jesus in all of human history! Instead, in many parts of the world, the church seems to be like the salt that has lost its savor (Matthew 5:13). Our homes, relationships, priorities, and lifestyles seem little different from the world's. Obviously, something is missing.

We must engage more and more Christians in the serious, life-changing process of becoming like Jesus. We need a clearer understanding of how to be true followers of Christ. We need a well-defined vision of the target for spiritual formation, as well as instruction in how we can practically move in that direction. We must embrace the awe and wonder of the opportunity we have to be transformed by God's love.

An Overview of *Relational Discipleship*

Chapter 1 of this course helps us to discover and begin living out God's purpose for our lives. Why are we here? What is our real significance? We will discover that we each have a crucial purpose related to the glory of God.

Chapter 2 explores the ways in which God the Father and God the Son love each other. We will see that the spiritual formation process mirrors this love relationship. This is critically important because spiritual formation is primarily *relational*—it involves Spirit-prompted relationships with both God and God's people. Chapter 2 will help us discover that we are loved in the same way the Father loves the Son, and that we can love God in the same way the Son loves the Father.

Chapter 3 affirms that we must actively participate in the process of spiritual formation. Philippians 2:12, 13 instructs us to "continue to work out your salvation with fear and trembling, for it is God who works in you to will and to act according to his good purpose." How can we practically cooperate with God? What is His part, and what is ours? Chapter 3 champions the concept of the "yielded walk," through which we respond to what God is doing as part of our responsibility in the process of spiritual formation.

Chapters 4, 5, and 6 urge us to walk in the light of three divine "light sources": God's Son, God's Word, and God's people. The process of spiritual formation should involve being led by the Spirit to walk consistently in all three sources of light, in order that we might better reflect the glory of God.

Chapter 7 explores the "worthy walk," shedding light on a critical result of the spiritual formation process—transformed character.

Finally, **Chapter 8** provides a fitting conclusion to the course and issues an ongoing challenge to walk in love as we experience transformation in our relationships.

Chapter 1

Life's Purpose Transformed

"When the Lord saw that he had gone over to look, God called to him from within the bush . . ." (Exodus 3:4).

magine Moses tending Jethro's flock alongside Mount Horeb. As he performs his familiar routine, he catches a glimpse of a burning bush out of the corner of his eye. Moses' absentminded gaze is soon replaced by an intensifying curiosity, then perplexity as he realizes that the bush is not surrendering to the flames. As Moses draws closer to the fireproof bush, the Most High God suddenly thunders forth from within it: "Moses! Moses!"

What if the Creator is calling you just as certainly as He called Moses? What if He has a clear, divine purpose for your life just as He did for Moses? Can you feel your heart tremble with astonishment and swell with shy delight as you imagine the Creator calling out *your* name?

Moses' brush with God's glory at Mount Horeb transformed his life, his sense of purpose, his people, and human history. Encounters with Jehovah are like that—we are never the same again. God revealed Himself to Moses in a bush that burned but did not burn up, and Moses responded. This simple principle—God reveals, God's people respond—will guide us as we explore our life purpose together.

> **This simple principle—God reveals, God's people respond—will guide us as we explore our life purpose together.**

What is Your Life's Purpose?

Why are you here? Why has the Creator put you on this planet?

Is the purpose of life simply to accomplish, acquire, and achieve as much as we can? Is it about having influence, financial security, or fun? Is our life purpose accurately expressed by the popular bumper sticker that asserts, "He who dies with the most toys wins"? Or is there more to life than these things?

The tragedy of September 11, 2001, changed the world, and undoubtedly many of us re-evaluated the question, "Why am I here?" My wife, Teresa, and I reflect often on where we were that day, just as you and countless millions of others do. We were glued to an airport television, en route to a retreat for ministry couples, when the first World Trade Center tower collapsed. Humankind's evil toward one another shook our world that day, but I believe that through it all, God was revealing Himself. The Spirit brought immediately to my heart Hebrews 12:26, 27: "'Once more I will shake not only the earth but also the heavens.' The words 'once more' indicate the removing of what can be shaken—that is, created things—so that what cannot be shaken may remain." We saw things shaken that day that we did not think could be shaken, and were reminded that, ultimately, only eternal things will remain.

More than two decades ago, I was personally shaken by an event that forced me to re-evaluate my life's purpose. A man in his late sixties, who had recently become a follower of Jesus, was speaking at a community-wide leadership event. He shared that as a young adult he had embraced the importance of financial security and the influence it would bring. He purposed that before he reached the age of 30 he would become a millionaire—and he did. He then set out in pursuit of other goals: becoming a multi-millionaire by age 40, seeing the world, and gaining prestige and power along the way. Although he was successful in achieving these new goals, he tragically lost his wife and family to divorce along the way. Next came more financial success, but a second broken home. A teenage daughter attempted suicide, and a son ended up in prison.

I can still remember the sobering impact of his next few sentences. As he reflected on his life, he said, "Early in life I purposed to climb the ladder of success, and from the world's viewpoint I climbed it! But when I got to the top, I looked around, and the ladder was leaning against the wrong wall."

Pause and Reflect

Is Your Ladder Leaning Against the Right Wall?

Pause to consider the fact that you and I are in some ways climbing our own ladders. We each do something with the 1,440 minutes of each day. We invest time, energy, and resources in some set of priorities. But how do these investments relate to eternity? There are many ladders to climb, many things to pursue. But we should be concerned with investing our lives in priorities that last—in things that "cannot be shaken."

Consider for a moment some of your top life priorities—the investments of your life that matter most.

As I look back on my life, I hope I have made a lasting investment in and impact on _____

_____

_____

_____

(For example: *my spouse; my children; those with whom I work; the professional field in which I work; my neighbors; my friends; my grandchildren; my church or ministry; a cause, project, or mission; those around me who do not know Jesus.*)

Share your responses with your partner or small group. As others share, you might want to make note of their responses. This will enable you to know one another better as you journey through *Relational Discipleship* together.

What a tragedy it would be if we discovered late in life that our ladder was leaning against the wrong wall! How can we know that our life priorities will stand the test of time? How can we be sure that our lives will be all that God intends?

We need clarity of vision—an eternal perspective on our life's purpose. Followers of Jesus have been called into His eternal kingdom (Colossians 1:13), and with this call comes a divine plan and purpose. In this course, we will explore the mystery of God's desire for your life and mine. How do your life priorities relate to His? How can you discover God's hope for your life? What is **He** longing to see happen through you and in you? We gain additional insight into these questions as we follow the biblical story of the glory of God.

THE STORY OF GOD'S GLORY: A CLUE TO OUR LIFE PURPOSE

Throughout its pages, the Bible tells the story of God's glory. The story begins with God walking and talking in the Garden with Adam (Genesis 2:15–20). Then, God is personally present with Abram, promising to birth a nation from his descendents, multiply them greatly, and deliver them from their oppressors (12:1–3; 15:1–16).

On the back side of the wilderness, Moses spots a bush that burns but is not consumed. The glory of God is present in that bush (Exodus 3:1–6). Moses becomes the human leader of the Israelites as they escape from bondage in Egypt, but they are **really** led by the glory of God, which appears as a cloud by day and a pillar of fire by night (13:21, 22).

God Initiates the Experience of His Glory.

Picture yourself as a young boy or girl traveling through the wilderness with Moses. Time and again, you observe supernatural phenomena that confirm God's physical presence in your midst. A mysterious cloud settles on the tabernacle, and the Lord pervades it with His glory, causing the cloud to burn with fire by night. You always halt your travels until the cloud or the fire lifts from the tabernacle.

With each divine disclosure, you become increasingly aware of the tangible presence of the Lord among you. Day after day and night after night, when God's glory moves, you move—God initiates, you respond.

Pause and Reflect

Your Testimony to His Initiative

Pause to consider the truth that God drew you into a relationship with Him at your "new birth," following this same simple pattern:

- He initiated: "'No one can come to me unless the Father who sent me draws him . . .'" (John 6:44).

- You responded: "For it is by grace you have been saved, through faith . . ." (Ephesians 2:8).

Reflect on your testimony:

- *God took initiative to reveal His Son, Jesus, to me by* _____
_____
_____ .

- *I responded by* _____
_____
_____ .

Further Manifestations of God's Glory

Later, after Moses has led you and the other Israelites out of Egypt, you see the glory of God descend upon Mount Sinai, accompanied by smoke, fire, thunder, and lightning (Exodus 19:16–19; 20:18–21; 24:15–17). Moses journeys up the mountain, where He receives the Ten Commandments. After another close encounter with God in which the Lord's glory passes before him (33:12–23), Moses returns to the people. The glory of God radiates from his face (34:29).

Picture Moses instructing you and your people to build a portable ark and tabernacle using the resources God has given to you. Then, at the precise moment when the consecrated priests are prepared, and the tabernacle, with all of its furniture and implements, is completed, the glory of God, manifested by His cloud, descends upon it (40:34–38).

After much wandering in the wilderness, and the occupation of the Promised Land under the leadership of Joshua, God's people encounter Him for centuries in the wilderness tabernacle. Then King Solomon is allowed by God to build a lavish, more permanent temple.

Now imagine that the day of the temple's dedication has arrived. As you watch God's high priests carry the Ark of the Covenant into that most sacred of places, the Holy of Holies, the expectancy and reverence of the people proves contagious, and the tension mounts as you wait longingly to see what will happen next. Suddenly, the cloud from the wilderness fills the temple, signifying the presence of the Lord, and His glory permeates the place. The intensity of His holy presence forces you to prostrate yourself before Him in worship and adoration as you rejoice in the midst of His glory once again (1 Kings 8:10, 11; 2 Chronicles 7:1–3).

Responding to God's Initiative

Before we move on, consider your heart's response to the truth that God always takes the initiative to reveal Himself to you. Just as He made Himself known through the burning bush and the pillars of cloud and fire, the Creator has revealed His Son to you, made you a part of His body, the church, and involved you by His Spirit in the process of being transformed by His love. What emotions touch your soul when you reflect on the wonder of these truths?

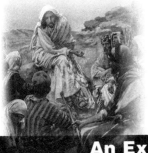

An Experience With God's Son

"God made him who had no sin to be sin for us, so that in him we might become the righteousness of God" (2 Corinthians 5:21).

Pause and consider Christ's cry to His Father from the Cross: "'My God, my God, why have you forsaken me?'" (Matthew 27:46)? As Jesus took our sin on Himself, the Father, in His holiness, had to turn away.

Reflect once more on being born again. Why did Christ become sin, or, more personally, for *whom* did He do it?

Quietly listen to His Spirit whisper the words to your soul: "He did it for you. He did it for you!"

The One who knew no sin became sin (2 Corinthians 5:21). If He did not need to die for any other person in the whole world, He would have died for you—and He *did* die for you!

Allow yourself to respond to this glorious truth. Meditate on the thought, or even whisper the words, "He did it for me." Is your heart moved with wonder, humility, and joy? Do gratitude and praise fill your soul?

Now share these feelings with God. Give thanks for His initiative in manifesting His glory and presence to you.

Lord, I am so grateful that _____

_____

_____

_____

_____

God's People Reject His Glory.

As time goes on, God's people compromise and go the way of the world. The kingdom is divided. Both Israel and Judah fall into immorality and idolatry, and eventually both are taken into captivity. From bondage in Babylon, the people of God inquire of the prophets, "Why have we been treated so? Why do we find ourselves in

> **The Israelites are in bondage because of their rebellion against God. He has withdrawn His presence. The glory is gone.**

captivity?" The prophet Ezekiel sees a vision depicting what has happened to them: "Then the glory of the Lord rose from above the cherubim and moved to the threshold of the temple. The cloud filled the temple, and the court was full of the radiance of the glory of the Lord. . . . Then the glory of the Lord departed from over the threshold of the temple . . ." (Ezekiel 10:4, 18).

God's chosen people are in captivity because they have failed to respond to the experience of God's glory among them. Thus, the glory of God is withdrawn from them, not because He really wants to leave them, but because their behavior demonstrates that they do not really want His transforming presence. The Israelites are in bondage because of their rebellion against God. He has withdrawn His presence. The glory is gone.

The Results of the Absence of God's Glory

Following the ministry of the prophet Malachi, the Lord's messengers fall silent. For the next four hundred years, people go to the temple at the appointed time to perform their religious duties, but the presence of God is gone. Year after year, decade after decade, they "go to church," but God is not there. Not surprisingly, the Pharisees rise to power during this period. The bondage of legalism arose in the context of the practice of religion apart from the presence of God.

God's Glory Returns

Fast forward to that chilly night on the hills outside Bethlehem. The shepherds are admiring the stars, when suddenly an angel of the Lord bursts forth from the sky. The shepherds are overcome by wonder and fear, robbed of speech and powers of description, and ". . . the **glory** of the Lord shone around them . . ." (Luke 2:9).

This appearance by the angels to the shepherds signals the return of the glory: "The Word became flesh and made his dwelling among us. We have seen his glory" (John 1:14). For 33 years, the glorious presence of God—which was previously in the bush, in the cloud, in the fire, on Mount Sinai, on the face of Moses, in the tabernacle, and in the temple—is displayed in the person of Jesus Christ.

Jesus is betrayed and dies a criminal's death on a cross. But the good news of the gospel is that, on that cross, He pays the penalty of sin. The One who has never known sin becomes sin, for a divine purpose—that we might become the righteousness of Christ through Him (2 Corinthians 5:21). He dies that we might **become**. Our calling is all about His hope of our becoming.

After three days, Jesus rises from the dead. For the next 40 days, He teaches His followers about the kingdom of God. He then ascends into heaven. But before He leaves, He tells His followers to wait in Jerusalem for the empowerment of the Holy Spirit (Acts 1:8).

Obediently, they gather, pray, and wait for ten days. Suddenly, a noise like a violent wind roars through the house, and tongues of fire descend from heaven and separate to rest on each disciple (2:1–4). The glory is back!

God's Glory—In Us

Until this point, the glory of God had dwelt in a bush, on the face of Moses, in a cloud, in a fire, in a tabernacle, in a temple, and in His divine Son. But now the glory dwelt somewhere that it had never been before Pentecost—inside created beings, inside God's children.

Scripture confirms this new home for the glory of God: ". . . Christ in you, the hope of glory" (Colossians 1:27). The glory of God, which was manifested among Moses and the Israelites and in the person of Jesus, now rests inside you and me. Christ in us represents God's greatest hope of making His presence known here on Earth.

LIFE'S PURPOSE: EXPRESSING THE PRESENCE OF GOD

The kingdom to which we have been called is a kingdom of God's glory. Our calling and purpose are directly related to His glory. We are here to make His glory known—to express the presence of God. He wants to be seen and known through us, just as He was seen and known in the tabernacle and the temple.

If God had consulted me about His plan for making His glory known on Earth, I am sure that I would have recommended another way. I might have suggested writing messages across the sky, or just having Jesus travel around in His resurrected, glorified body, walking through walls and showing up in churches and communities. I do not think I would have approved of the idea of God entrusting His presence, His glory, to mere mortals like you and me. But God, in His wisdom, *did* choose us to bear and express His glory. ". . . Christ in you, the hope of

> **We are here to make His glory known—to express the presence of God. . . . He has entrusted His glory to me. He has entrusted His glory to you!**

glory." He has entrusted His glory to me. He has entrusted His glory to you!

Pause and Reflect

Pause to consider the truth that the Creator has a definite hope and desire for your life. His heart is longing to engage you in His divine purpose.

What thoughts and feelings do you have about being trusted as a bearer of God's glory? (Check as many as apply to you.)

_____ *I feel blessed to enjoy such an awesome privilege.*

_____ *I feel inadequate for the responsibility.*

_____ *I am afraid that I will make God look bad.*

_____ *I need to know more about what it means and how I can live it out.*

_____ Other: _____

Complete the following sentence:

As I consider God's hope for me and reflect on the privilege of being home to the very glory of God, I feel . . . _____
_____
_____
_____
_____

HOW CAN WE FULFILL THIS PURPOSE?—THE WONDER OF HIS GRACE

You are the home for God's glory. You are to bear and express the glory of God wherever you go. ". . . Whether you eat or drink or whatever you do, do it all for the glory of God" (1 Corinthians 10:31). His hope of glory, the prevailing evidence of His divine presence, is in you. But how are we to consistently live in a way that allows His glory to shine forth?

By God's Grace, We Were Chosen to Bear His Glory.

What did Moses do to earn the privilege of bearing witness to dramatic displays of God's glory?

What did the people of Israel do to deserve the honor of having God's glorious presence dwell among them?

What have **we** done to make ourselves worthy of being trusted to express God's glory?

The answer to all of these questions is, "Absolutely nothing!"

Grace is God's unmerited favor toward us. It is given not because of anything we have done, but simply because God longs to give it (Isaiah 30:18). By grace, He extends His love to us, showers us with blessings, and imparts purpose to our lives, in order that His glory might be displayed through us.

> **What have we done to make ourselves worthy of being trusted to express God's glory? Absolutely nothing!**

God's grace enlisted Moses and delivered and guided Israel. His grace persevered through Israel's unfaithfulness. It was by His grace that the glory returned that night in Bethlehem. It was His grace that embraced us: "For it is by grace you have been saved . . ." (Ephesians 2:8).

So what is the evidence of God's presence in our lives? Are we to look for the fire? The cloud? The shine on our face? No—any of these would in some way call attention to us, rather than to Him. It is His grace—His unmerited favor, His undeserved love—that testifies most clearly of His presence.

Gratefulness for His Grace Empowers Us to Live as Glory-bearers.

Gratefulness is the only appropriate response to this grace we have experienced. Unfortunately, as Israel so tragically demonstrated, gratefulness for the grace of the presence of God is far from automatic. Even we, as Christians, who carry the glory of God within us, can take His grace for granted.

But as we reflect on the truth that Christ in us is the hope of glory, gratitude should be our prevailing emotion. We need not feel a sense pressure, obligation, or duty. Instead, we should embrace the wonder of it. The Creator has graced us with the privilege of joining Him in making Himself known here on Earth. He wants you and me to experience the ". . . joy inexpressible and full of glory" (1 Peter 1:8 NASB) that comes from a life of receiving and giving grace—a life in which we never get over the wonder that, by His grace, we have been loved, and in which we are excited to share that same grace with others.

What a God we serve, what a joy we possess, what a gift and a privilege to experience genuine relationship with the God of the universe! May the name of the Lord be worshipped, glorified, and praised! May His holy presence fill us each day so that we may venture forth as His living epistles to love and to serve in the name of our God.

RESULTS OF FULFILLING OUR CALLING

The *Relational Discipleship* course is intended to equip us to live out the awe-inspiring purpose of expressing the glory of God. As we make this journey together, what results may we expect?

The Glory of God's Grace Will Be Praised.

"He predestined us to adoption as sons through Jesus Christ to Himself, according to the kind intention of His will, to the praise of the glory of His grace, which He freely bestowed on us in the Beloved" (Ephesians 1:5, 6 NASB).

This verse, which describes so eloquently God's loving initiative toward us, reveals an important result of fulfilling our purpose and calling: Wherever God's grace is displayed, the glory of His grace will be praised. Every demonstration of His unmerited love in our lives presents us with an occasion for offering Him our heartfelt praise.

In addition to prompting praise in our own hearts, our recognition of God's grace will bring Him glory among those who hear our testimony. One of our challenges is to honestly explore and reveal the pain, tragedies, trials, betrayals, and failures of our lives, in order to demonstrate the glorious grace of the One who brought us through those times and loved us even in the midst of troubles of our own making. Such grateful testimony to the wonder of His grace brings Him praise.

How Displaying Grace Prompts Praise to God
In our frequent role as conference speakers, my wife, Teresa, and I often share stories about our own marriage journey that illustrate the glory of God's grace. Teresa will usually tell about our honeymoon. "We were married at age 16, neither of us being Christians" she might say by way of introduction, "and at that age, one of us didn't have much sense." (You can probably guess which one of us that was.)

Teresa usually goes on to tell about the morning after our wedding night. That morning, my buddy, Stanley, knocked on our motel room door and invited me to go play pool. Teresa was still asleep, so I figured she wouldn't mind—the pool hall was just a couple of blocks down the road after all—so I went with Stanley to shoot some pool, leaving my new bride alone.

People often come up to me after Teresa shares this tragic story and ask, "Why do you let her tell that story? It makes you look like a jerk!" I understand that, but I always tell them, "When she's telling that story, you need to understand what is going on inside of my heart. I'm not feeling embarrassed, guilty, or ashamed. I'm feeling overwhelmed by the grace of the God who has healed that terrible hurt. I'm awed and overjoyed that God has brought complete forgiveness and restoration."

How did my wife forgive my insensitivity? How was Teresa's acceptance of me restored? How was trust restored to our relationship? Only by the grace of God. So I want her to tell that story (and many others) because they inspire praise of the glory of His grace.

An Experience With God's Word

"To the praise of the glory of His grace . . ." (Ephesians 1:6 NASB).

Pause to reflect upon your experience of the glory of God's grace, recently or in the more distant past. Be still before the Lord and ask His Spirit to stir up remembrances, perhaps of times when . . .

- He unexpectedly provided for you.

- He accepted you in the midst of a failure.

- He healed your physical or emotional pain.

- He restored a broken relationship.

Complete the following sentence:

I give thanks and praise to God for the grace He gave me when _____
_____
_____
_____.

Share your completed sentence with your partner or small group. Then pray together, expressing further thanks and praise to God.

The Glory of God's Kingdom Will Be Expanded.

A second result of fulfilling our purpose as bearers of God's glory is the expansion of His kingdom. As we come to understand that the kingdom is about Him, not us, we will recognize

His heart, His passion, His love for people. As we realize that the Christian life is about bringing glory to Him, things like evangelism, discipleship, and missions will no longer be religious activities that we do just in order to feel better about ourselves or to earn God's approval. Instead, these things—indeed, all forms of ministry—will represent opportunities to express and expand God's glory!

> **As we realize that the Christian life is about bringing glory to Him, things like evangelism, discipleship, and missions will no longer be religious activities that we do just in order to feel better about ourselves or to earn God's approval. Instead, these things—indeed, all forms of ministry—will represent opportunities to express and expand God's glory!**

Some of us are familiar with church environments in which it is understood that if you are really spiritual, you will not only come to every weekend and mid-week service, but you will also come when the "super saints" gather for organized evangelism or early-morning prayer. If you are going to be a **real** Christian, you must consistently and faithfully participate in every church-related activity, regardless of whether it is generally considered "required" or "optional."

Tragically, in such environments, the expansion of the glory of the kingdom is often reduced to an endless string of activities which we use as a basis for comparing ourselves with others. This

> **Our calling is about His presence, about His glory, about His kingdom.**

often leads us to become either smugly self-congratulatory or critical and condemning of those who don't quite measure up. The Christian life thus becomes just another self-focused enterprise.

Our calling is about **God's** presence, about **His** glory, about **His** kingdom. Yet if we are honest, we must all admit that on some level, we are wondering, *What about me?* In Matthew 16:25, Jesus says, "'. . . Whoever loses his life for me will find it.'" One of the keys to finding your calling and purpose is to become so absorbed by His presence, His glory, and His kingdom that you lose yourself, and thus find your life.

We Find Life's Purpose by Fulfilling Christ's Great Commission.

". . . Go and make disciples of all nations . . ." (Matthew 28:19) is Christ's invitation to join Him in making His glory known here on Earth. As we express the glory of God, His Spirit is at work, challenging people to notice and turn aside, just as Moses did when he saw the burning bush. They will want to know, "What is that? Where did you get that love, that acceptance, that compassion, that grace?" Our only explanation is that we got it from God. The calling that He has placed on our lives is evidence of the grace that He has extended to us.

> There are demonstrations of God's glorious grace in your life. He wants to send people your way who want to know, "What is that?"

As a husband who has made so many mistakes, imagine my wonder at the fact that, by His grace, Teresa and I recently celebrated 40 years of marriage. Having started by abandoning my wife for my pool-shooting buddy on our honeymoon, how is it possible that I now share deep closeness and abundant love with this same lady 40 years later? How could that have happened? It only happened because of the glory of His grace. I cannot get over the wonder of such grace.

There are similar demonstrations of God's glorious grace in your life. He wants to send people your way who will want to know, "What is that?" There is no doubt that what he is doing in Teresa and me through the calling He has on our lives is

> How will you so live and love that the glory of God's presence is manifested among those you long to impact?

partially for the benefit of other leaders, couples, and families. When other people notice the evidence of His presence in our marriage and ask, "Where did you get that acceptance?" or "Where did that spirit of forgiveness come from?" or (more bluntly) "How did you put up with that jerk, Teresa?" there is but one true response we can offer: It was only made possible by His glorious grace.

Consider again the life priorities you previously identified. Are your spouse, children, family members, and friends being compelled to turn aside and notice the glory in your life? Is your workplace, profession, community, or ministry being impacted by His presence in you? How will you so live and love that the glory of God's presence is manifested among those you long to impact?

An Experience With God's People

Expressing the Glory of His Grace

"As each one has received a special gift, employ it in serving one another as good stewards of the manifold grace of God" (1 Peter 4:10 NASB).

Consider for a moment the "manifold" or "multi-faceted" grace of God of which Peter speaks in this passage. God's grace—His unmerited favor—has, at times, been expressed toward you as . . .

- acceptance when you have failed (Romans 15:7).

- encouragement when you were down (1 Thessalonians 5:11).

- support when you have struggled (Galatians 6:2).

Then pause to ask God, *"How could I better express the glory of Your grace to others?"* Ask Him specifically about how better to express acceptance, encouragement, and support. Listen—be still. Recall from earlier in this chapter who it was that you said you hoped to impact. Allow God's Spirit to reveal who needs to receive His glorious grace through you. Then complete the following sentences:

I could better express God's . . .

- *acceptance to* _____.

- *encouragement to* _____.

- *support to* _____.

(For example: *I could better express God's acceptance to my son. I tend to be critical of most of what he says or does. I need to stop focusing on the negative and start telling him that no matter what he says or does, I still love him.*)

(For example: *I could better express God's encouragement to my wife. She tends to get discouraged, and I could let her know that I recognize and appreciate her gifts and abilities.*)

"And let us consider how we may spur one another on toward love and good deeds" (Hebrews 10:24).

With vulnerability and sincerity, share with your partner or small group what God has revealed to you. Then pray, specifically asking that God's Spirit would express His grace through you so that others will turn aside to see Him in you. Offer simple yet specific prayers, such as the following:

Heavenly Father,

Please help me to be more accepting of _____. Please show me how to do this in practical ways.

In Jesus' name, Amen.

Pause to Pray

Close your time together with the following prayer:

Heavenly Father,

I pause to consider the wondrous truth that Your Holy Spirit has taken up residence in me, and the awesome privilege I have to reflect Your glory. In all aspects of my life, I see expressions of Your undeserved favor, unmerited love, and incomprehensible grace. May these outpourings of grace continually prompt praise from my heart. I understand that through the person and power of Your Holy Spirit, I have the potential to so express Your presence that others around me would wonder, "What is that? Why is that happening?" May I honestly answer that what they see is not the result of my goodness, but of Your grace.

As I pray and reflect on this, may my heart be challenged with the words of Jesus: "Whoever loses his life for me will find it." Father, would You give me the revelation of what you are going to do in me as I come to focus first on You? Would You introduce to me the wonder of the truth that I can be an expression of the very presence of God? Would You unveil by Your Spirit more and more of the mystery of "Christ in me, the hope of glory"?

In Jesus' Name, Amen.

After He was raised from the dead, Jesus announced, "'. . . As the Father has sent me, I am sending you'" (John 20:21). In Chapter 2, we will explore the questions, "How did the Father send the Son?" and "How is He now sending us?" We will explore the mystery of the love that is expressed and experienced within the Trinity and discuss the significance that the coming of this same transforming love to dwell in **us** has for our spiritual formation.

CHAPTER 1 FOLLOW-UP PROJECTS

1. **Ministry Skill:** Developing Your Personal Testimony
2. **Life Application:** Sharing the Glory of His Grace
3. **Scripture Memory:** 1 Corinthians 10:31; Colossians 1:27

Ministry Skill

Developing Your Personal Testimony

". . . Always being ready . . . to give an account for the hope that is in you . . ."
(1 Peter 3:15 NASB).

As others begin to witness God's glory expressed through our lives, and to "turn aside" like Moses did at the burning bush, we must be ready! The testimony of the first century church was that people ". . . took note that these men had been with Jesus" (Acts 4:13). Living out the glory of His grace will cause those around us to notice that we also have been with Him.

First comes our "walk" with Him, and then our "talk" of Him. Being prepared to talk of Him can begin with our personal testimony of coming to know Him at our new birth. Reflect on the time when you received Him as Savior and submitted to Him as Lord. Then complete the following sentences:

- My life before receiving Christ can be described as . . .

- Some of the events leading up to my salvation included . . .

- Some of the people God used in my life to draw me to Himself included . . .

- Some of the changes that God's Holy Spirit began to make in my life over time included . . .

- I'm thrilled to describe my relationship with Him today as . . .

After reflecting on these responses, you might wish to write out your testimony in narrative form, being prepared to share it as God provides opportunities.

Life Application

Sharing the Glory of His Grace

". . . Faithfully administering God's grace in its various forms" (1 Peter 4:10).

Imagine being given a multi-faceted diamond with many aspects to its brilliance and worth. God's grace is just such a priceless, many-sided gift!

Imagine that one facet of His grace is His **acceptance** and that we have the opportunity and privilege to share it with others. "Accept one another, then, just as Christ accepted you, in order to bring praise to God" (Romans 15:7).

To whom did you previously indicate that you might better express God's acceptance? Write that person's name here: _____

Accepting this person might involve . . .

- giving him/her another chance when something has been done wrong.

- allowing him/her to think, act, or feel differently from you.

- loving him/her in spite of offenses.

- speaking words like:
  "What you did was wrong, but I still love you and want a relationship with you."
  "We do think differently on that issue, but I still want to be your friend."
  "No matter what you do, I will always love you."

Pause to consider how this person might receive God's gracious acceptance through you— how might you freely give it this week?

The Lord has impressed me to give His acceptance in a special way this week to _____
by _____.

Now imagine that another facet of God's grace is revealed as you encounter His **encouragement**. Maybe while reading the Word, you are reminded by the Spirit that "'through . . . the encouragement of the Scriptures we might have hope" (Romans 15:4), and challenged to ". . . encourage one another and build each other up . . ." (1 Thessalonians 5:11).

To whom did you previously indicate that you might better express God's encouragement? Write that person's name here: _____

Encouraging this person might involve . . .

- making a phone call, writing a card, or sending an email to check on him/her.

- promising to pray for him/her and then actually praying on a regular basis.

- spending personal time with him/her in order to hear what he/she is working on, and then urging persistence toward the goal.

- speaking words like: *"You can do it!"*
  "I believe in you and in what God is doing in you."
  "Keep at it—I know you can succeed!"

Pause to consider how this person might receive God's gracious encouragement through you—how might you freely give it this week?

The Lord has impressed me to give His encouragement in a special way this week to

_____
by _____.

Next, imagine that God turns the beautiful "grace diamond" ever so slightly to reveal yet another facet of His grace: His **support**. "Bear one another's burdens, and thereby fulfill the law of Christ" (Galatians 6:2 NASB). The law of Christ is the law of love, and He has first loved us by bearing the burden of our sins upon the Cross.

To whom did you previously indicate that you might better express God's support? Write that person's name here: _____

Supporting this person might involve . . .

- noticing that he/she is under stress and then giving specific help (such as bringing a meal, doing work around the house or office, assisting with a move, running errands, or providing child-care) in order to alleviate it.

- speaking words like: *"I can tell you are under stress, and I'd like to help. I've got three hours tomorrow afternoon. What could I do to support you?"* (If the answer is uncertain, suggest some possibilities.)

Pause to consider how this person might receive God's gracious support through you—how might you freely give it this week?

The Lord has impressed me to give His support in a special way this week to _____ by _____.

You have now identified three aspects of God's glorious grace that He could share through you. His glory is resident in you. You can now express the glory of His grace to the people you have identified.

In the next seven days, would you make at least one of these possibilities into reality? After you do, share what God has done in and through you with your partner or small group when you meet again.

Scripture Memory

1 Corinthians 10:31
"So whether you eat or drink or whatever you do, do it all for the glory of God."

Colossians 1:27
"To them God has chosen to make known among the Gentiles the glorious riches of this mystery, which is Christ in you, the hope of glory."

Chapter 2

The Secret of Spiritual Transformation

"I have become [the church's] servant by the commission God gave me to present to you the word of God in its fullness—the mystery that has been kept hidden for ages and generations, but is now disclosed to the saints. To them God has chosen to make known among the Gentiles the glorious riches of this mystery, which is Christ in you, the hope of glory" (Colossians 1:25–27).

The Greek word *musterion*, which is twice translated as "mystery" in the passage above, does not refer to something that is frightening or inexplicable, but rather to something that was previously hidden but has now been divinely revealed. The glory of God, which had vanished from among the Israelites for four centuries, was manifested in the world for 33 years in the person of Christ and was then entrusted to those in whom He dwells. As followers of Jesus, we now have the opportunity to make known "the glorious riches of this mystery."

In this chapter, we will consider how Christ manifested God's glory and how we can do the same. In order to provide the context for a deeper understanding of these matters, we must first examine both the nature of our intimate relationship with God and the nature of the unique relationship between the Father and the Son.

GOD'S PLAN FOR RELATING WITH HUMANITY

The intimate relationship between God and His children is one in which God always initiates, and we are given the opportunity to respond. In Chapter 1, we discussed the way in which God takes the initiative in revealing His glory to humankind, and explored our hearts' responses to the wondrous truth that we have become bearers of that glory. Now we will see that God's loving initiative toward us was first manifested at creation, that it was demonstrated in the sending of His Son, and that it remains a constant theme in God's relationship with each of His children. This perpetual cycle of God's initiative and man's response provides us with key insights into the process of spiritual formation.

> **The intimate relationship between God and His children is one in which God always initiates, and we are given the opportunity to respond.**

God's Initiative to Create

"The Lord God formed the man from the dust of the ground and breathed into his nostrils the breath of life, and the man became a living being" (Genesis 2:7).

"God . . . breathed . . . and man became. . . . " In these few words, we find the first scriptural reference to God's relationship with humankind. During the first five days of creation, the Creator simply spoke things into existence, but here, on the sixth day, He *relates*. God breathes, initiating the Spirit's activity, and man becomes. To be ". . . created in the image of God . . ." (Genesis 1:26) is to be created with the capacity to respond to and relate intimately with the Creator.

God's Initiative to Redeem

How was this ability to relate intimately with God affected by the Fall of Man? It was forfeited. Man became spiritually dead: "Once you were dead, doomed forever because of your many sins. You used to live just like the rest of the world, full of sin, obeying Satan . . ." (Ephesians 2:1, 2 NLT). Spiritual death means separation from God—apart from Christ, man has no ability to relate intimately with his Creator.

But the good news—the gospel—is that, even though ". . . sin entered the world through one man [Adam], and death through sin . . ." (Romans 5:12), ". . . the last Adam became a life-giving spirit" (1 Corinthians 15:45 NASB). Christ, as the "last Adam," came to give life and to restore the intimacy of relationship with God that was lost in the garden. Once again, God took the initiative by sending His Son, and mankind was given the opportunity to respond.

God's Initiative to Reveal

Our ability to experience spiritual formation—the divine process by which we become like Jesus—also depends upon God's initiative. God is constantly seeking to reveal Himself to us in various ways, and His Spirit works within us to empower our response. Let me share a personal testimony as an example of the way this can work.

I had traveled to Tennessee, to the International Headquarters of one of the denominations we serve through the Great Commandment Network. Following a long day of ministry meetings, I made my way down the hall with my friend, John. Still ahead of me that evening was a two and a half hour drive to Atlanta for a dinner meeting, to be followed by staff planning for the next day.

As John and I neared his office doorway, he inquired, "Would you like to come in and visit for a few minutes before you head off?" Gracious Southern hospitality and our close friendship were behind the invitation. My initial internal response was something like, "The last thing I need to do is to sit down with John. I have a long drive and more meetings still ahead of me!"

> **My answer startled me, not only because it had come so quickly (in response to what seemed like divine prompting), but also because of the choice of words: "I need to." What did that mean? In my human understanding, sitting down to visit was the last thing I "needed" to do.**

But suddenly I felt an unexplainable peace and a sense of clear direction in my spirit. "Sure," I said, "I think I need to." My answer startled me, not only because it had come so quickly (in response to what seemed like divine prompting), but also because of the choice of words: "I **need** to." What did that mean? In my human understanding, sitting down to visit was the last thing I "needed" to do.

All of this transpired in just a brief moment, with John being completely unaware of my internal dissonance. We went into his office, sat down, and began to chat. No more than two or three minutes had passed before the phone rang. John got up and moved to his desk to answer it.

I looked across the room and recognized from John's facial expression and tone of voice that he was hearing some troubling news. On the other end of the line was John's mother-in-law, making her first phone call after learning from her doctors that she had a brain tumor. John slumped down into his desk chair. They talked about things like how to inform the family— who would tell her daughter, John's wife Sue? How and when should they share the news with her grandchildren, including John's three daughters?

I moved across the room and put my hand on John's shoulder. When he put down the phone, he stood up, and we embraced. I prayed and offered comfort. This was why I "needed" to be there! Had I not stayed, the God of all comfort would still have been there to care for John, but He wanted me to join Him in this holy task!

As John and I walked back across the room to discuss the call further, a verse of Scripture suddenly rose up in my heart. Genesis 18 records how God came to earth in the form of a man to visit His friend Abraham. As He prepares to destroy the wicked cities of Sodom and Gomorrah, the Lord pauses and asks Himself, "'Shall I hide from Abraham what I am about to do?'" (Genesis 18:17). It seems that God was longing to let Abraham in on His plans.

> **On many other occasions, God has taken the initiative in various ways in order to reveal something important to me, but this particular experience stirred in me a deep longing for more.**

As I recalled this passage, my skin began to tingle. More tears filled my eyes, but they were different from my previous tears—not tears of sorrow for a hurting friend, but tears of wonder, gratitude, and awe. In the hallway only a few minutes earlier, God had let me in on what He wanted to do through me! On many other occasions, God has taken the initiative in various ways in order to reveal something important to me, but this particular experience stirred in me a deep longing for more.

John's mother-in-law has since been touched by the Great Physician. I join with the many who have offered praise to the Lord for His healing grace, and I am additionally grateful because the impact of that day in John's office still lingers in my heart. The experience birthed within me a longing for God to reveal more of Himself, more of His ways and His plans. I yearn to hear His voice.

What about you? Are there times when you experience an unexplainable yet undeniable witness of God's Spirit in your heart and recognize that He has just revealed something to you? As you pray, read the Word, and experience genuine fellowship with other Christians, are you sometimes filled with wonder and awe as you realize that God has just spoken to your spirit? How long has it been since you have felt that God was revealing something specifically to you? Perhaps you feel (as I did that day in Tennessee) that it has been too long.

An Experience With God's People

". . . The Lord . . . takes the upright into his confidence" (Proverbs 3:32).

Consider a time in your life when you sensed God revealing something to you—when you felt that He "took you into His confidence." It may have occurred as you encountered Scripture, as you were praying, or as you listened to the sharing of another. Then complete the following sentence, either on your own or using one of the sample beginnings listed below.

I remember having a very personal encounter with God when He . . .

- *drew me to Himself by . . .*

- *gave specific direction concerning . . .*

- *provided caution/warning about . . .*

- *revealed Himself as . . .*

- *confronted me concerning . . .*

- *affirmed/encouraged me concerning . . .*

- *reassured me during . . .*

(For example: *"I remember having a very personal encounter with God when He encouraged me concerning my worth to Him. I felt like a failure, but I sensed the Lord saying to me, "'I love you. Don't give up, keep trying!'"*)

"And let us consider how we may spur one another on toward love and good deeds" (Hebrews 10:24).

Experience this scripture by sharing your testimonies of God's revelation with your partner or small group. Rejoice together as the Lord encourages your deepened walk with Him.

THE WONDER OF INTRA-TRINITARIAN LOVE

Christ's Final Prayer

In Christ's final prayer with His disciples(John 17:1–26), He refers to the wondrous mystery of the love that exists within the Trinity. Scripture tells us that ". . . God is love" (1 John 4:8), and that He is ". . . abounding in love" (Psalm 103:8), but how is this love manifested within the Trinity, particularly between the Father and the Son? The answer to this question holds significant insight into the divine plan for our spiritual formation.

Christ's Final Prayer Reveals His Desire for Us.

Christ's prayer was not only for those who were present in the upper room. It was for all those who would later come to believe in Him as Savior, including you and me (John 17:20). In the prayer's final verse, Jesus reveals His heart's desire for us: "'I have made you known to them, and will continue to make you known in order that the love you have for me may be in them and that I myself may be in them'" (v. 26). Thus, Christ prays that you might have in you both the Father's love for the Son ("that the love you have for me may be in them") and Christ Himself ("that I myself may be in them"), including His love (as the Son) for the Father.

The Answer to Christ's Prayer

Jesus' prayer is answered for the 11 disciples at Pentecost and for every believer at the moment of salvation. Consider that at your new birth, much more happened than you may have realized! One of this chapter's Follow-up Projects will explore what it means that we have been given ". . . everything we need for life and godliness . . ." (2 Peter 1:3) and blessed ". . . with every spiritual blessing in Christ" (Ephesians 1:3). One of the most amazing blessings we have been given is this: We have received both the Father's love and the Son's love, which serve as the standard for all other love relationships.

> **The very same love that Jesus and the Father experienced within the Trinity is now in us. This is part of what it means for God's glory to dwell in us.**

The Father's Love and the Son's Love

The very same love that Jesus and the Father experienced within the Trinity is now in us. This is part of what it means for God's glory to dwell in us. But how can we truly experience this "intra-Trinitarian" love? And what are the implications of our experience of it for our spiritual formation? To answer these questions, let us take a closer look at the unique ways in which the Father loves the Son and the Son loves the Father.

The Father Loves the Son by Revealing.

Nowhere in Scripture does the Son reveal anything to the Father. But frequently, the Father demonstrates His love for the Son by revealing things to Him: "'For the Father loves the Son and shows him all he does . . .'" (John 5:20).

Picture Jesus as a child, growing ". . . in wisdom and stature, and in favor with God and men" (Luke 2:52). How did He grow in wisdom? Who taught Him? Did not the Father express His love by revealing to Jesus what would make Him wise?

> **Nowhere in Scripture does the Son reveal anything to the Father. But frequently, the Father demonstrates His love for the Son by revealing things to Him: "For the Father loves the Son and shows him all he does" (John 5:20).**

The Father demonstrated love for the Son by revealing to Him both the shame of the crucifixion and the joyful results of it: ". . . Who for the joy set before him endured the cross, scorning its shame . . ." (Hebrews 12:2). Picture the garden scene, as Christ, in anguish, prays fervently, and His sweat falls like drops of blood to the ground (Luke 22:44). He looks into the cup of the sin of all mankind, past, present, and future. He entrusts Himself to His Father, yet asks, "'Father, if you are willing, take this cup from me . . .'" (v. 42). But the Father does not take the cup. The Son is to drink it all. The One who has never known sin, who was ". . . tempted in every way, just as we are—yet was without sin" (Hebrews 4:15) is to become sin. Yet is it not possible that, at the same time, the Father was revealing the ultimate joy of redemption and resurrection?

Pause to consider that the Holy Spirit, in response to Christ's upper room prayer, has placed within you this same self-disclosing love of the Father. You have within you One who is longing to reveal to you all things! "'When he, the Spirit of truth, comes, he will guide you into all truth. . . . He will bring glory to me by taking from what is mine and making it known to you'" (John 16:13, 14). The same divine initiative that breathed into Adam is now available through the Holy Spirit to breathe within you.

The Son Loves the Father by Yielding.
Nowhere in Scripture do we see the Father yielding to the Son. Indeed, the Father is always the one who commands, sends, and commissions the Son. And the Son, as a demonstration of His love, always yields to the Father. Consider the following statements of Jesus from the Gospel of John:

> **Nowhere in Scripture do we see the Father loving the Son yielding to Him, but the Son, as a demonstration of His love, always yields to the Father.**

- "'. . . I love the Father and . . . I do exactly what my Father has commanded me'" (John 14:31).

- "'If you obey my commands, you will remain in my love, just as I have obeyed my Father's commands and remain in his love'" (15:10).

- "'I can do nothing on My own initiative. . . . I do not seek My own will, but the will of Him who sent Me'" (5:30 NASB).

- "'The Son can do nothing by himself; he can do only what he sees his Father doing, because whatever the Father does the Son also does'" (5:19).

- "'. . . I . . . speak just what the Father has taught me'" (8:28).

Jesus' commitment to yield was so strong that He described it as His very nourishment: "'My food . . . is to do the will of him who sent me and to finish his work'" (4:34).

In response to the Father's revealing, the Son yields. His yielding is so complete that Jesus says, "'. . . Anyone who has seen me has seen the Father . . .'" (14:9). He perfectly represents His Father's will, ways, and heart.

Both the Father's Revealing Love and the Son's Yielding Love Are Dwelling in You.
In accordance with the desire that Christ expressed in John 17:26, you have received, in the person and presence of the Holy Spirit, both the Father's revealing love and the Son's yielding love. Through the Spirit's empowering, the love that exists between the Father and the Son is working in you to restore the intimacy with God that Adam and Eve forfeited in the garden.

The love that dwells within us is fundamentally an "others-focused" love. Even before the creation of man, the Father and the Son in some sense extended love to "another" in the context of their unique, eternal relationship within the Trinity. And, of course, we too have been recipients of God's "others-focused" love: "'For God so loved the world . . .'" (John 3:16); ". . . God demonstrates his own love for us . . . " (Romans 5:8).

Having now been given the responsibility and privilege of serving as bearers of this "others-focused" love, we must express it in practical ways to those near us—our spouses, children, family members, friends, and anyone else we encounter in the course of our daily lives. We have the wondrous opportunity to express love to others in the same way that Jesus did—by receiving the Father's revelation and yielding to it.

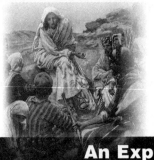

An Experience With God's Son

". . . He always lives to intercede for them" (Hebrews 7:25).

Pause to reflect on the fact that, as the One who knows all things, Christ is aware that both His love and the Father's love are dwelling in you—but He is also aware that you do not always fully experience and express the Father's revealing love and the Son's yielding love.

Now imagine Christ laboring in prayer, interceding for His people. More personally, picture Him praying for you. Imagine that you are there to witness Him praying, as the disciples often did. As you approach Jesus, you hear Him fervently praying for the needs of your life. Then you hear Him groan as He pleads with the Father on your behalf: "As one who has received My Spirit, this child has Your revealing love within. You are speaking, Father, but this child of Yours is not hearing You. I long for this one to hear You. Please open this heart and mind, and give this child the desire to yield to whatever You say."

What does it do to your heart to know that Jesus, your Savior and Lord, loves you so much that He is interceding for your needs and praying that you might hear Him and yield to Him?

Tell the Lord what you are sensing in your heart:

As I consider that You are praying for me—for the needs of my life and that I might hear You more clearly—it brings _____ to my heart.

(For example: *joy, peace, gladness, thanks, excitement, awe,* or *wonder.*)

Pause to pray, worshiping the Lord with gladness (Psalm 100:2). Share with Him your thanksgiving and praise.

RESPONDING TO GOD'S IN-DWELLING LOVE: THE SECRET OF SPIRITUAL TRANSFORMATION

Genuine spiritual transformation begins as we recognize and embrace our purpose as those in whom the glory of God dwells—to express and extend His presence. We have the privilege of manifesting God's glory in the same manner that Jesus did—by receiving the Father's revelation and yielding to it.

As we have seen, within us as believers are both the Father's revealing love and the Son's yielding love. The Son was "sent out" on our behalf by the Father and empowered by the Spirit to perfectly yield to His Father's revealing love. We also have been sent out: "'. . . As the Father has sent me, I am sending you'" (John 20:21). In the person of the Holy Spirit who abides in us, God initiates the revealing and empowers the yielding.

> **We have the privilege of manifesting God's glory in the same manner that Jesus did—by receiving the Father's revelation and yielding to it.**

Spiritual Transformation Requires Receiving What God Reveals.

"'. . . He who loves me will be loved by my Father, and I too will love him and show myself to him'" (John 14:21).

The Father demonstrates His love by revealing His Son, speaking through His Word, and ministering through His people. In order to be transformed into His image ". . . from glory to glory . . ." (2 Corinthians 3:18 KJV), we need to take full advantage of these three sources of God's revealing "light." Like young Samuel in the temple of God, the cry of our hearts should be, ". . . Speak, Lord, for your servant is listening . . ." (1 Samuel 3:9). The true disciple longs to receive from God through . . .

- the light of His Son: "'I am the light of the world . . .'" (John 8:12).

- the light of His Word: "Your word is a lamp to my feet and a light for my path" (Psalm 119:105).

- the light of His people: "'You are the light of the world . . .'" (Matthew 5:14).

As God's children abundantly receive from His Son, His Word, and His people, they are enabled to more clearly hear Him. Chapter 3 of *Relational Discipleship* explores in more depth how to hear God and receive what He reveals. Chapters 4, 5, and 6 then explore how we as disciples can learn to walk in these three sources of light in order to receive all the Lord has for us.

Spiritual Transformation Requires Yielding to What God Reveals.

"'Whoever has my commands and obeys them, he is the one who loves me . . .'" (John 14:21).

Through the gracious work of the Holy Spirit, the hearts of those who have experienced God's transforming love are inclined to yield, yearning to please the One who has revealed Himself to us, longing to express and extend God's glory. The follower of Christ longs to testify, as Christ did in His final hours: "'I have brought you glory on earth by completing the work you gave me to do'" (John 17:4).

Spiritual Transformation Requires Yielding Before Receiving.

We have been brought into the same love relationship as that of Jesus and the Father. Fully devoted followers of Christ are not transformed by knowledge acquired, activities engaged in, or events attended. Spiritual transformation—the process of being shaped into the likeness of Jesus—is brought about by hearing what God reveals and yielding to it. But is there anything else we can observe about Jesus' commitment to yield to His Father's will?

Recall Jesus' anguished prayer at Gethsemane. Had the Father already revealed all that Jesus would go through in the Crucifixion? Certainly Jesus knew that His earthly "temple" would be destroyed and then "rebuilt" in three days (John 2:19). Jesus told His disciples that He ". . . must suffer many things and be rejected by the elders, chief priests and teachers of the law, and that he must be killed and after three days rise again" (Mark 8:31). But did Jesus really know the full magnitude of the suffering that He was about to experience?

Christ knew that He was going to die to pay the penalty for the sin of mankind, but did the One who had never known sin, who was "tempted in every way . . . yet was without sin" (Hebrews 4:15), know that He was about to "become sin"? Did He really understand the implications that had for His relationship with the Father? Having existed in relationship with the Father for all eternity, could He foresee that, at Calvary, He would experience aloneness for the first time? Did He know that, as He "became sin," the Father would turn away from Him? Did He anticipate the pain this rupture would bring, the pain that would prompt Him to cry out, "'My God, my God, why have you forsaken me?'" (Matthew 27:46).

Is it possible that the Son was not certain that He had received His Father's final answer? That might explain why He prayed, "'My Father, if it is possible, may this cup be taken from me . . .'" (26:39). But consider His next words: "'Yet not as I will, but as you will.'" Herein lies the secret to spiritual transformation: Jesus was committed to yield even before He really understood to what He was yielding. And once the Father's will was made clear, Jesus was determined to obey, as illustrated by His words to Peter: "'Shall I not drink the cup the Father has given me?'" (John 18:11).

In our flesh, we often want to know first, so we can make an informed decision about whether we want to yield. But true disciples who are eager to experience the transforming love of God will embrace a different approach:

> **"'Yet not as I will, but as you will.'" Herein lies the secret to spiritual transformation: Jesus was committed to yield even before He really understood to what He was yielding.**

- First, we commit to yield by faith, relying on the Holy Spirit.

- We then listen, seeking to hear God's voice and discern His will.

- As "knowing" comes, we uphold our commitment to yield by following God's direction.

- Finally, we are sent out to reveal what we have received, in order that others may, in turn, yield.

Once again, the young Samuel should serve as our example—we are to be listening servants, committed to yield and longing to hear.

An Experience With God's Word

"'If anyone chooses to do God's will, he will find out whether my teaching comes from God or whether I speak on my own'" (John 7:17).

Our commitment in faith to yield to God before we fully know is the secret to spiritual transformation. Like Jesus, we must say, "'Not as I will, but as you will'" (Matthew 26:39).

Are you committed to yield in this way? Is it your very "spiritual food" to do the Father's will (John 4:34)?

We invite you by faith to pray a prayer of yielding—to give expression to your heart's commitment to yield to whatever God asks of you, even when you do not really understand what He is asking or what He is doing.

Consider the circumstances of your life right now. Think about your important relationships. Reflect upon critical situations and unanswered questions. What are you struggling with right now?

Compose your own prayer of commitment to yield, and then offer it to God. Use the structure below to assist you as needed.

Father, before I even hear your voice concerning . . .

- *my calling . . .*

  as a husband to _____
  as a wife to _____
  as a parent to _____
  as a friend to _____
  as a _____ *to* _____

(For example: *my calling as a parent to demonstrate the importance of personal purity regarding what I allow to come into my mind.*)

- *the decision regarding . . .*

(For example: *the decision regarding how to best care for our aging parents.*)

- *how I should handle . . .*

(For example: *how I should handle the conflict with my boss.*)

- *what I should trust You for relative to . . .*

(For example: *what I should trust You for relative to my health problem and the treatment for it.*)

. . . I yield to You all that I am, and all that my future holds. By faith, I commit to live out what You reveal. Speak, Lord, Your servant listens.

After you have offered your prayer and spent some time listening for the Lord, share your prayer with your partner or small group. Pray for one another, asking God to answer your prayers, and to empowering each of you to live out your commitment to yield.

CHAPTER 2 FOLLOW-UP PROJECTS
1. **Bible Doctrine:** The Blessings of Your New Birth
2. **Bible Study:** The Father Reveals
3. **Bible Study:** The Son Yields
4. **Scripture Memory:** John 17:26

Bible Doctrine

The Blessings of Your New Birth

"Praise be to the God and Father of our Lord Jesus Christ, who has blessed us . . . with every spiritual blessing in Christ" (Ephesians 1:3).

Much more than you likely ever imagined took place when you yielded to Jesus Christ, who was revealed to you as Savior and Lord, the sinless Son who took upon Himself your sin at Calvary.

At that moment, God provided you with a great number of unique and permanent blessings.

The following is a list of the things God does for each believer at the moment of salvation.

You may well find other blessings that could be added to the list. It is valuable and important that we understand thoroughly our relationship with the Lord, particularly all the things He did for us the moment we entered into a relationship with Him. Meditate quietly before the Lord, asking His Spirit to speak through His Word about these blessings and what they mean to you.

The moment you received Christ as your Savior and were born again . . .

- your spirit, once dead, was made alive (Ephesians 2:1–5).

- you were declared His child (John 1:12; 1 John 3:1).

- you were invited to come boldly before Him for more of His grace (Hebrews 4:16).

- you were chosen to be in the eternal plan of God, sharing the destiny of the Lord Jesus Christ (Ephesians 1:4, 5).

- you were reconciled (brought into relationship) with God (2 Corinthians 5:18; Ephesians 2:14–18; Colossians 1:19, 20).

- you were redeemed (purchased from the "slave market" of sin) (Romans 3:24; Ephesians 1:7; Colossians 1:14; 1 Peter 1:18).

- you were (and are) no longer condemned by God (John 3:18; 5:24; Romans 8:1).

- you came under God's grace; You are no longer under His judgment (Romans 3:24–28; 1 John 2:1, 2).

- you were adopted (placed as an adult heir) into the family of God (Romans 8:15–17, 23; Ephesians 1:5).

- you were justified (declared righteous), and thus made acceptable to God (Romans 3:24; 5:1; 8:30; 1 Corinthians 6:11; Titus 3:7).

- you were regenerated (spiritually reborn) (John 3:3–8; Titus 3:5).

- you were forgiven all your sins—past, present, and future (Ephesians 1:7; 4:32; Colossians 1:14; 2:13, 14; 3:13).

- you were delivered from the kingdom of Satan (Colossians 1:13).

- you were brought near to God and made a citizen of His kingdom (Ephesians 2:13, 19; Philippians 3:20; Colossians 1:13).

- you were freed from your slavery to sin; You were enabled to yield to God, obeying Him out of a desire to love Him (Romans 6:17, 18).

- you were purified and made eager to do what is good (Titus 2:14).

- Jesus was praying for you (Romans 8:34; Hebrews 7:25).

God's Holy Spirit came to live within you—to guide you, convict you, comfort you, teach you, minister to others through your spiritual gifts, and make evident the glory of the Father's revealing love and the Son's yielding love (John 14:15–17, 26; 16:7–15; 1 Corinthians 12:27–31).

As you consider these tremendous expressions of God's loving heart for you, ask yourself this question: What did you do to earn or deserve these blessings and gifts?

In order to gain these benefits of my salvation, I did the following: _____
_____

Do you have anything written on the lines above? Is there anything that you could have done to earn them? "He saved us, not because of righteous things we had done, but because of his mercy . . ." (Titus 3:5).

What do you feel in your heart as you consider that, not only did God love you so much that He did all of the above for you, but He delighted in it? How does it make you feel to realize that He was passionate in His love for you and eager to give you these blessings, which you could never have gained by your own efforts?

Dear God, as I consider these truths revealed to me by You in Scripture—as I reflect on all that You did for me when You saved me, as I think on all the many blessings You have bestowed because of Your infinite love for me—my heart is stirred with _____
_____.

Now express your willingness to yield to what He has revealed to you:

Lord Jesus, just as You yielded to Your Father in all things, I also wish to yield to You. Just as the Father has loved You, You have loved me. Thus I choose right now to yield to You concerning _____
_____.

Continue to reveal to me who I am in Your eyes and how You have blessed me and will continue to bless me.

In Your name, Amen.

Bible Study

The Father Reveals

". . . He is intimate with the upright" (Proverbs 3:32 NASB).

Throughout Scripture, we see that it is God's nature to reveal. The "upright" are those who yield to what He reveals.

Pause to pray for God to freshly reveal Himself to you:

Dear God, I long to hear from You. Please show me more of You—Your deeds, Your ways, Your thoughts, Your heart, and Your character. Amen.

THE DISCLOSURE OF GOD

Explore the following scriptural truths concerning God's disclosure of Himself to you. Allow your heart to be stirred with gratefulness for the fact that God longs for you to know Him. Then record your thoughts concerning what God has revealed according to these Scriptures.

- Psalm 19:1–6; Romans 1:20
  God has revealed Himself in _____.

- Psalm 103:7
  God has revealed both His _____ and His _____.

- 2 Timothy 3:16, 17
  God has revealed Himself through _____.

- Exodus 14:26–31
  God revealed His _____ when He parted the Red Sea and destroyed the Egyptian army.

- Isaiah 40:21–26
  God has revealed His absolute _____ over all things.

- 1 Timothy 2:3, 4
  God has revealed His desire that _____ be saved.

- Romans 1:17; 3:21–24
  God has revealed how to be brought into a relationship with Him that does not depend upon our righteousness, but upon our receiving His _____ through _____ in Jesus Christ.

- Romans 5:8
  God's _____ is revealed in this: While we were still sinners (not after we had made ourselves acceptable), the Son of God, Jesus Christ, died for us.

- Romans 1:18, 19; 2 Corinthians 5:10
  God has revealed that there will be an ultimate accounting—a final _____ that all mankind will face.

- James 1:5
  God will reveal _____ to us if we ask for it.

- John 14:9
  God the Father is revealed in the person of _____.

- Revelation 21–22
  God has revealed the glorious future destiny of His people, who will dwell with Him for all the rest of _____.

FORGET NONE OF HIS BENEFITS.

- Write out a special prayer of thanksgiving to God, praising Him for stirring within you a fresh appreciation for these many aspects of His revelation.

- Praise the Lord for the wondrous truth that His nature is to disclose Himself to us.

- Praise Him that, rather than remaining hidden, He has chosen to let us know Him in all these different ways.

- Ask Him to "take you into His confidence."

Dear God, Thank You for revealing _____.

I praise You for _____.

Father, I long to hear You more clearly, and to love You more dearly. Please reveal to me more of _____
_____.

In Jesus' name, Amen.

Bible Study

The Son Yields

"And Jesus cried out again with a loud voice, and yielded up His spirit" (Matthew 27:50 NASB).

In His last words from the Cross, Christ expresses both His identity and His legacy to us: He yields!

This is the key that unlocks the mystery of Jesus and the Father being One: The Son did only what He had seen His Father doing. He spoke only what He had heard His Father speak.

Meditate on the following Scriptures, which testify of the ways in which Jesus yielded. Then record your thoughts concerning how Jesus yielded, or to what Jesus yielded.

Jesus yielded . . .

- to be born in a _____ (Luke 2:7).

- to leave heaven's riches and become a _____ (Philippians 2:5–8).

- to Joseph and Mary's parental _____ (Luke 2:51).

- to _____ in His humanity (Luke 2:52).

- to be _____ as we are (Hebrews 2:18; 4:15; Luke 4:1–13).

- His own _____ to the Father's (John 5:19, 30).

- to _____ authority (John 19:1–22).

- to the authority of _____ (Luke 4:4, 8, 12).

- to the Father's _____ in Gethsemane (Matthew 26:39, 42, 44).

"'I am the Lord's servant,' Mary answered. 'May it be to me as you have said'" (Luke 1:38).

Meditate now on the simple power of Mary's immediate willingness to yield to the angel's announcement that she, a virgin, would give birth. Though it was inexplicable, required inestimable sacrifice and faith, and was sure to bring ridicule from others, she still yielded.

Now consider some of the issues and areas of struggle in your life. In which of these areas might the Lord be longing to see you yield?

I sense the Lord specifically prompting me to yield to Him concerning _____
_____
_____.

Now conclude your study by offering this prayer, expressing your choice to yield to the God who has revealed Himself to you:

Lord, thank You for showing me where I need to yield to You. Not my will, but Your will be done. Give me the faith, strength, and courage to do what You have asked of me by the power of Your Spirit.

In Jesus' name, Amen.

Scripture Memory

John 17:26

"'I have made you known to them, and will continue to make you known in order that the love you have for me may be in them and that I myself may be in them.'"

Chapter 3

Transformed Priorities

"Meanwhile his disciples urged him, 'Rabbi, eat something.' But he said to them, 'I have food to eat that you know nothing about'" (John 4:31, 32).

Jesus' disciples had just returned from grocery shopping in the Samaritan town of Sychar. They knew that Jesus had not eaten before they left, so they were surprised when He refused to eat what they had brought Him and wondered where He could have gotten the food of which He spoke. Imagine their increased perplexity when He added, "'My food . . . is to do the will of him who sent me and to finish his work'" (v. 34).

In the previous chapter, we explored the foundational principle that the love of God works within the believer to **reveal** His ways, His truth, and His will, and to empower us to **yield** to what He reveals. In this way, God has both initiated His presence in us and entrusted us with expressing His presence to others.

In this chapter, we will introduce principles for nourishing this life in the Spirit. Just as certainly as we must consume physical food in order to mature physically, so also we must be nourished spiritually if we are to mature as faithful disciples. For Christ to be formed in us, we, too, must come to crave the spiritual food of seeking God's will and doing His work, just as Jesus did.

As we faithfully follow Christ, our human desires to accomplish, acquire, and achieve are replaced by a divinely prompted longing to hear God and yield to Him. The hunger for spiritual nourishment, prompted by the Holy Spirit within us, reorders our priorities.

> Just as certainly as we must consume physical food in order to mature physically, so also we must be nourished spiritually if we are to mature as faithful disciples.

HUNGER TO HEAR AND YIELD

Hunger to Hear What God Reveals

"'But what about you?' he asked. 'Who do you say I am?' Simon Peter answered, 'You are the

Christ, the Son of the living God.' Jesus replied, 'Blessed are you, Simon son of Jonah, for this was not revealed to you by man, but by my Father in heaven. . . . On this rock I will build my church . . .'" (Matthew 16:15–18).

Notice that when Christ affirms Peter, He highlights the Father's revealing, and He affirms Peter for hearing the Father's revelation. It is as if Jesus is saying to Peter, "You got it! And the reason you got it is because the Father revealed it to you." Both the Father's revealing and Peter's yielding are acknowledged. This foundational process of God revealing and His followers yielding—hearing and responding—is the "rock" upon which Christ is even now building His church.

Consider your own new birth and the ways in which God revealed Christ to you. Perhaps He did this through . . .

- the spoken witness of others concerning the reality of Christ in their lives.

- the unspoken witness of Christ-centered lives lived before you.

- the witness of Scripture, as God's Word came alive to you in its revelation of Christ.

- the proclamation of the "good news" by a pastor, evangelist, or other servant.

Regardless of how it came about, the Father revealed His Son to you, giving you the opportunity to yield to Him.

Hunger to Yield to What God Reveals
". . . Everyone who calls on the name of the Lord will be saved" (Romans 10:13).

As previously noted, the "food" that nourished Jesus was to yield to whatever His Father revealed. Just as we frequently hunger for physical nourishment, we must become hungry to yield to God.

Perhaps this is what the beatitude speaks of: "'Blessed are those who hunger and thirst for righteousness, for they will be filled'" (Matthew 5:6). Could this righteousness that leads to the satisfaction of hunger be the tangible expression of disciples yielding to what they have heard from God?

When the Father revealed Christ to you for salvation, you yielded; you responded with trusting faith. You may have come to see your hopeless state and yielded to Christ as your only hope. You may have come to see Christ as the source of life eternal and yielded to His abundant life. In any case, you, like Peter, were challenged to yield to the reality of what the Father was revealing to you—that Christ was who He claimed to be and that you desperately needed Him.

Often, I share the impact that the life and testimony of my grandfather Jerry had on me. I was a rebellious teen with a fast car. I made frequent 30-mile trips to the junior college I attended, and my high-speed commutes led to six speeding tickets in six months. Knowing that my license was in jeopardy, my granddad arrived one Sunday afternoon with a plan: "David," he said, "I think those policemen know you and your car so well that they are just waiting each day to see which one of them gets to give you the next ticket. I've come up with an idea. Why don't you start driving my pick-up truck so they won't know it's you?"

> **The accepting presence of God working through Granddad touched me that day. The glory of God was in that pick-up truck, drawing me to turn aside and consider Christ.**

The next morning, I headed off to school, excited about the opportunity to scam the police. But I soon found that Granddad knew something about that old pick-up that I did not know. That truck would not go over the speed limit!

As I realized what he had done, my emotion was not irritation or anger—I smiled and began to laugh. And then this rebellious teen, with some religious exposure but no relationship with God, had this strange thought: "If there's a God, He'll be a lot like Granddad." I needed someone to accept me, not reject me, even in the face of my rebellion. In that moment, a strange warmth came over me, followed by tears of appreciation for Granddad.

Forty years later, I say it like this: the accepting presence of God working through Granddad touched me that day. The glory of God was in that pick-up truck, drawing me to turn aside and consider Christ. God was revealing Himself and prompting me to consider yielding to Him.

An Experience With God's People

"So then, just as you received Christ Jesus as Lord, continue to live in him" (Colossians 2:6).

Think about how God revealed Jesus to you to bring you to salvation. Did He reveal Christ through Scripture? Did He reveal Christ through the testimony of changed lives by those around you? Did He meet you and reveal Himself to you directly? How did you "hear" Him?

In what ways did you yield to His revealing? What did your yielding to this revelation "look like"?

Christ was revealed to me for who He really is through _____
_____
_____.

My yielding to Him involved _____
_____
_____.

(For example: *Christ was revealed to me for who He really is through the gentle and gracious example of my grandfather. My yielding to Him involved a life transformation in which I stopped rebelling and began pursuing Him.*)

Take the time to share with one another the initial encounter with Christ that brought you into His kingdom. Then rejoice together "to the praise of the glory of His grace . . ." (Ephesians 1:6 NASB).

Close by reflecting on Colossians 2:6: ". . . As you have received Christ Jesus the Lord"—by God's revealing and your yielding—"so walk in Him" (NASB). Have a time of group prayer, praising God for the grace that enabled your salvation and asking Him for more revelation to which you might yield.

Heavenly Father, thank You for revealing to me Your Son. Praise You for the grace that has brought countless blessings to me as I have yielded to You. Please continue to reveal Yourself to me, as I continue to yield myself to You.

In Jesus' name, Amen.

LONGING TO HEAR

"Very early in the morning, while it was still dark, Jesus got up, left the house and went off to a solitary place, where he prayed" (Mark 1:35).

Both the religious leaders of Christ's day and His own followers often misunderstood His priorities. Surely, the disciples thought, Jesus would not want to be distracted by children. Yet He rebuked the disciples and welcomed the children with open arms (10:13–16). Surely, the Pharisees reasoned, a respectable teacher should have nothing to do with publicans and sinners, yet Jesus was known as their friend (Matthew 11:19). Throughout His life on earth, Christ displayed countercultural priorities, giving time and attention to people and things that others despised, rejected, or deemed unimportant.

The rationale behind Jesus' behavior becomes perfectly clear when we understand the greater, overarching priority that guided Him: His insistence on hearing from His Father. "'I can do nothing on My own initiative . . .'" He declared (John 5:30 NASB). The actions that so confounded the Pharisees and disciples alike give evidence that Jesus' conduct was guided not by man's opinions, but by His Father's heart. Paradoxically, the God-Man Jesus, the eternally existent One through whom everything holds together, freely admitted His humble dependence upon His Father—and thus, His need to hear His Father.

> **Hearing the Father must become our pursuit and passion, just as it was the Savior's.**

Scripture records that Jesus frequently spent time in solitary prayer in order to more clearly hear the Father's voice. While this practice should have served as a model for the disciples, it appears that they sometimes had a different set of priorities. On one occasion, when they realized that Jesus had gotten up early and left the house, "Simon and his companions went to look for him, and when they found him, they exclaimed: 'Everyone is looking for you!'" (Mark 1:36, 37). In the disciples' minds, there were more pressing concerns for Jesus to address—crowds to be greeted, lessons to be taught, miracles to be performed. But Christ's first priority was to hear His Father. So it is for the faithful disciple. Hearing the Father must become our pursuit and passion, just as it was the Savior's.

The Pursuit of Hearing Him

Our pursuit of hearing God shapes key aspects of our spiritual life:

Bible Study

As true disciples, we long not for mere knowledge but for His Word to become for us ". . . living and active . . ." (Hebrews 4:12). We desire to be nourished by the Word—to "'. . . not live on bread alone, but on every word that comes from the mouth of God'" (Matthew 4:4). Chapter 4 will examine our calling to walk in the light of God's Word and explore the necessity of experiencing Scripture for effective spiritual formation.

Worship
We long to enter into God's presence with thanksgiving and praise (Psalm 100:4). But as disciples, our entering serves a deeper purpose: We long to hear from Jesus, ". . . the author and perfecter of our faith . . ." (Hebrews 12:2). Chapter 5 will explore our calling to walk in the light of Christ. We will see that spiritual formation requires consistent experiences of Christ as He really is.

Fellowship
We long not to impress others, but to be impacted by them as the Spirit speaks to us and ministers to us through them. "As iron sharpens iron, so one man sharpens another" (Proverbs 27:17). Expressions of Christlikeness in others provide an example, often revealing areas of needed growth and prompting change in us. Chapter 6 will explore our calling to walk in the light of God's people as a third critical element of our spiritual formation.

The Discipline of Solitude
Passion to hear God is practically expressed through the discipline of solitude: "'Be still, and know that I am God . . .'" (Psalm 46:10).

When solitude—time alone with Jesus—becomes our priority . . .

- prayer becomes listening as well as asking.

- meditation on Jesus nurtures our spirit.

- withdrawal from the world and connection with Jesus frees us to "Set [our] minds on things above, not on earthly things" (Colossians 3:2).

- victory in the battle of the mind is experienced as ". . . we take captive every thought to make it obedient to Christ" (2 Corinthians 10:5).

Solitude moves us beyond a preoccupation with His blessings to intimacy with the One who blesses. Religious practice gives way to the experience of His presence. (Chapter 5 will give additional practical suggestions concerning spending time alone with Jesus.)

Solitude moves us beyond a preoccupation with His blessings to intimacy with the One who blesses.

Overcoming Spiritual Deafness: Putting Away Anything That Hinders Hearing

Convinced that the Good Shepherd is speaking to us, His sheep, we should now long to be assured that we are hearing Him clearly. The true disciple passionately pays any price to hear from God—not out of duty or obligation, but rather out of longing for communion with the Shepherd.

"In the year that King Uzziah died, I saw the Lord . . ." (Isaiah 6:1). The prophet Isaiah's dramatic encounter with the Lord brought with it the need to put away his sin. First, he confessed the sin: "'Woe to me!' I cried. 'I am ruined! For I am a man of unclean lips, and I live among a people of unclean lips . . .'" (v. 5). Then God cleansed Him by sending an angel with a burning coal. The angel touched Isaiah's mouth and said, "'See, this has touched your lips; your guilt is taken away and your sin atoned for'" (v. 7).

What happened next? Isaiah heard the voice of God saying, "'Whom shall I send? And who will go for us?'" Isaiah then yielded, saying, "'Here am I. Send me!'" (v. 8).

Cleansing precedes clarity concerning God's voice and will. Faithful disciples so long to hear the Lord that they, like Isaiah, seek to put away anything that might hinder hearing Him.

Sin

We are urged to ". . . get rid of all moral filth and the evil that is so prevalent . . ." (James 1:21), and to rid ourselves of ". . . all malice and all deceit, hypocrisy, envy, and slander of every kind" (1 Peter 2:1). Genuine confession of our sins to God brings the certainty of His promised forgiveness and cleansing (1 John 1:9). Putting away sin may also require confessing to those we have wronged (James 5:16).

Unresolved Emotions

We need to become free to live and hear God in the present. As our hearts become free from

such things as guilt, anger, bitterness, condemnation, and fear, we are better able to experience
". . . the peace of Christ . . ." ruling in our hearts (Colossians 3:15).

> **Cleansing precedes clarity concerning God's voice and will.**

- **Guilt** is to be confessed to God and to those we have hurt (1 John 1:9; James 5:16).

- **Anger and bitterness** are to be put away, as we express our gratefulness for God's forgiveness by forgiving others in turn (Ephesians 4:31, 32).

- **Condemnation** is to be replaced by gratitude for the glorious truth that ". . . there is now no condemnation for those who are in Christ Jesus" (Romans 8:1).

- **Fear** is to be removed by the perfecting of the love of God, the One who holds the future (1 John 4:18).

Childish Things

"When I was a child, I talked like a child, I thought like a child, I reasoned like a child. When I became a man, I put childish ways behind me" (1 Corinthians 13:11).

- Childish justifying must be replaced by personal accountability (Romans 14:12).

- Childish over-talking is to be superceded by increased listening—first to God, then to others (James 1:19).

- Childish self-preoccupation should give way to living out God's "others-centered" love (Philippians 2:3, 4).

On a recent Great Commandment Radio program, my wife, Teresa, recounted an instance of her own childish self-preoccupation early in our marriage:

"One day, after having worked many long days without a break, David expressed a desire for a much-needed day off. 'I'm really looking forward to just being able to relax tomorrow,' he said. My response, sadly, was, 'I wish I ever got a day off.' I not only hurt David with my comment, but I also revealed how focused on myself I was."

As Teresa vulnerably shared this testimony with the radio audience, I was reminded of how grateful I am for her maturity in Christ. For many years now, the "others-focused" love of Christ has prompted her to say, "I'm glad you'll have time off. You need it."

Self-Initiative/Confidence in the Flesh

We must wait patiently for the Spirit's initiative. "That which is born of the flesh is flesh, and that which is born of the Spirit is spirit" (John 3:6 NASB).

Self-initiative must be put away in favor of waiting to hear from the Lord: ". . . For You I wait all the day" (Psalm 25:5 NASB). Our thoughts and ways must be replaced by His higher ways: "'For my thoughts are not your thoughts, neither are your ways my ways . . .'" (Isaiah 55:8).

An Experience With God's Word

"Search me, O God, and know my heart; test me and know my anxious thoughts. See if there is any offensive way in me, and lead me in the way everlasting" (Psalm 139:23, 24).

Be still before the Lord and offer the same prayer that David prayed as you seek to put away the things that might hinder you from hearing God:

- *Search me, O Lord, for **sins** that hinder me from hearing You. Free me from all moral filth, evil, malice, deceit, hypocrisy, envy, and slander. Free me to have a cleansed heart and mind. Speak now, Thy servant listens.*

I need to put away _____.

- *Search me, O Lord, for **unresolved emotions** that keep me from hearing You. Free me from any guilt or condemnation, any anger or bitterness, any fear or anxiety. Free me to live each moment "in the present" with You. Speak now, Thy servant listens.*

I need to put away _____.

- *Search me, O Lord, for **childish things** that distract me from hearing You. Free me from rationalizing my behavior and blaming others, from idle chatter and self-focus. Free me to practice personal responsibility before You and others. Speak now, Thy servant listens.*

I need to put away _____.

*Search me, O Lord, for areas of **self-initiative** that prevent me from hearing You.*

- *Free me from my thoughts, **my** ways, **my** ideas, and **my** goals. May I instead embrace **Your** thoughts, **Your** ways, **Your** ideas, and **Your** goals. Speak now, Thy servant listens.*

I need to put away _____.

Pause and wait before the Lord. Listen as He reveals what needs to be put away.

Now yield to Him, even though you may not fully know all that will be necessary:

Lord, I sense the need to put away _____
from my life. Even before fully knowing all that may be required, I yield to You. I long to hear You. Remove this from my life so that I can more freely hear what You reveal to me.

In Jesus' name, Amen.

THE PRIVILEGE OF RESPONDING

". . . Today, if you hear his voice, do not harden your hearts . . ." (Hebrews 3:7, 8, 15; 4:7).

Just as Isaiah encountered the Lord, put away the sin of his "unclean lips," and then heard God's call, so also the faithful disciple prioritizes encounters with God, puts away all encumbrances to hearing, and seeks to hear more.

Subsequent chapters of this resource will address how we can hear God by receiving the light He gives us. But the key issue for now is this: Along with God's revelation comes the challenge to respond. As we hear His voice through His Word, through fellowship, or through listening prayer, we must choose to yield rather than hardening our hearts.

God certainly wants us to obey Him as He reveals Himself. But more is needed. Though obedience is necessary to walk uprightly with Him, it is not sufficient for true discipleship. Our obedience is to be empowered by a longing to please Him. Discipleship is not mere dutiful obedience; it must include a relational passion to please God.

> **Discipleship is not mere dutiful obedience; it must include a relational passion to please God.**

Too often, we as Christians can simply go through the motions, outwardly complying with external standards of right and wrong, while being motivated only by duty or obligation. Of the Israelites in Isaiah's day, God said, "'These people come near to me with their mouth and honor me with their lips, but their hearts are far from me'" (Isaiah 29:13). Likewise, the Pharisees sought after obedience to the Law, yet their hearts were far from God (Matthew 15:7–9). True disciples not only obey God with their actions, but draw near to Him with their hearts.

More Than Obedience: A Testimony

"Let us fix our eyes on Jesus . . . who for the joy set before him endured the cross . . ." (Hebrews 12:2).

Recent reflections in my own life challenged me to reconsider my understanding of obedience. I had come to be somewhat pleased with myself because of how I had helped Teresa over the years with her luggage as we traveled together. It first began years ago. After loading my luggage in the trunk for another trip to the airport, I noticed that Teresa had rolled her bag to the rear of the car, and then without comment took her seat in the passenger's side. Apparently, she wanted me to load her luggage for her. This became customary—I assumed this role of service, thinking that I was pleasing my wife and probably also bringing God great delight.

Next came airport security checkpoints. Teresa would make her way through security after putting her coat and purse on the security belt, leaving me to trip over her suitcase. Apparently, she expected that I would be glad to lift her bag onto the security belt for her, which I dutifully did.

Inside the aircraft, Teresa would take her seat, coat and purse in hand, and I would trip over her carry-on bag in the aisle. Again, I would spring to her rescue, quickly lifting her bag into the overhead bin and then putting mine in beside it. But my dutiful obedience was occasionally pushed beyond any reasonable limits of servanthood when, after being seated, I would hear the dreaded words, "Honey, I forgot to get my magazines out of my bag. Would you mind getting them for me?" With all the graciousness I could muster, I would comply. I would then assure myself that only a very few husbands would serve their wives as willingly and sacrificially as I did.

Then one day, I was preparing an Easter message, using as my text Hebrews 12:2: "Let us fix our eyes on Jesus . . . who for the joy set before him endured the cross. . . ." Suddenly, the

Holy Spirit seemed to say, "David, you're serving your wife with her suitcase, but where is your joy in doing it? Teresa sees your obligatory, dutiful compliance, but she also senses your occasional frustration and irritation, rather than My joy."

God had revealed to me my lack of passion for serving my wife. It was then important for me to yield. He had given me the example of His Son's joy through His Word, and His Spirit then began to prompt and empower my yielding. As a result, joy has now come to my "luggage ministry." Teresa is more pleased, and perhaps God is also.

Obedience Redefined

Our motivation for yielding to God should be an inner longing to please Him. By way of our new birth, we have within us One who longs to please the Father. Responding to God's revealing is thus a privilege, a gracious wonder by which we can find joy in pleasing Him, regardless of what may be required.

". . . Jesus . . . for the joy set before him endured the cross, scorning its shame . . ." (Hebrews 12:2). Jesus scorned the shame of Calvary because of the joy of pleasing His Father. The obedience that nourished Him (John 4:34) was rooted in this joy of doing the Father's will.

Would it have been genuine obedience if Christ had lived a perfect outer life, enduring the Cross, but was irritated by having to do so? Outward obedience without a joy-filled longing to please may not be real obedience. Is it possible that our obedience is only pleasurable to God when it is motivated by the joy of pleasing Him?

In the middle of His upper room prayer for the disciples and all those who would believe through their testimony, Christ requested, "'. . . that they may have the full measure of my joy within them'" (John 17:13). Without this joy of pleasing the One who has called us, dutiful obedience can still lead to hardened hearts. Signs of this "hardening" include . . .

> **Is it possible that our obedience is only pleasurable to God when it is motivated by the joy of pleasing Him?**

- a preoccupation with merely "doing" Christianity, rather than truly being Christlike.

- the substitution of religious activities, events, and knowledge for God's edifying love.

- the distortion of spiritual disciplines whereby they become channels through which we seek to seize God's blessings, or grounds for self-exaltation or self-condemnation.

Christ loved the Father through His joy-filled yielding. So can we, through the prompting and power of the One within us. May we exhibit not just willful, dutiful obedience, but obedience grounded in the joyful wonder that we, the created, get to bring pleasure to the Creator!

How to Cultivate Obedience Motivated by the Joy of Pleasing God

- Thank God often that you have received, in the person of the Holy Spirit, a yielding love.

- Declare to Him often that you long to please Him.

- Express joy for the privilege you have to express His glorious presence, and for the fact that He, through you, finds pleasure.

- Exercise yielding through submission in relationships with others. (For more on this important topic, see the Follow-up Projects for this chapter.)

An Experience With God's Son

"'. . . If we ask anything according to his will, he hears us. And if we know that he hears us—whatever we ask—we know that we have what we asked of him" (1 John 5:14, 15).

Return to Christ's upper room prayer, where He prays not only for the 11 remaining disciples, but also for "'. . . those who will believe in me through their message'" (John 17:20). One of His many requests in this prayer is ". . . that they may have the full measure of my joy within them" (v. 13).

This is His will for the disciples, and for you and me. He has revealed to us His desire—that we may be filled with His joy. It is time to respond, to yield.

Pray together with your partner or small group, expressing your heart's desire to yield to what God is revealing, and to do so joyfully, with an eagerness to please Him:

Lord Jesus, I desire for Your joy to be made full in me. I want my nourishment to be obedience to all You reveal to me, motivated by the amazing privilege of bringing joy to You, my Savior, Lord, and King. May Your Spirit in me motivate and empower me to please You with my life.

In Your name, Amen.

The faithful disciple gives priority to a lifestyle of walking in these simple principles of hearing and yielding. We have received Christ Jesus as Lord, and must now continue to live in Him (Colossians 2:6), receiving nourishment through our interactions with God's Word, God's Son, and God's people.

The psalmist declares, "In your light we see light" (Psalm 36:9). Our flesh has no light in itself, only darkness. It is the light, the revelation of God, that will nourish us into maturity and form the character of Christ in us. In the next chapter, we will explore one important source of this light—God's Word. We will discover that we gain spiritual nourishment as we receive and yield to the truths found in Scripture.

CHAPTER 3 FOLLOW-UP PROJECTS
1. **Bible Study:** The Priority of Hearing God
2. **Spiritual Discipline:** Exercise in Yielding (The Discipline of Submission)
3. **Scripture Memory:** John 4:34

Bible Study

The Priority of Hearing God

"As Jesus and his disciples were on their way, he came to a village where a woman named Martha opened her home to him. She had a sister called Mary, who sat at the Lord's feet listening to what he said. But Martha was distracted by all the preparations that had to be made. She came to him and asked, 'Lord, don't you care that my sister has left me to do the work by myself? Tell her to help me!' 'Martha, Martha', the Lord answered, 'you are worried and upset about many things, but only one thing is needed. Mary has chosen what is better, and it will not be taken away from her'" (Luke 10:38–42).

In this passage, we see a contrast between Martha, a follower of Jesus who truly loved Him but made a priority of **activity for Him,** and another follower, Mary, who loved Jesus and made a priority of **hearing from Him.**

Review the text and consider the following questions, along with the implications the passage might have for your own priorities:

1. What was Mary's posture? What is its significance to the principle of yielding even before you hear?

2. What was Mary's purpose?

3. Which priority does Jesus say is more important: listening to Him or doing things for Him?

4. What emotions does Martha seem to portray in her words to Jesus?

5. What evidence of self-centeredness, a demanding attitude, and an insistence on divisive comparison do you see in Martha's words and actions?

6. How might things and activities have crowded your own relationship with Jesus?

7. How might following Mary's example of prioritizing hearing from Jesus guard us against some of the fleshly distractions that stole Martha's joy?

Close your study with this prayer:

Lord Jesus,

I yield my priorities to You. I know that I need to prioritize hearing from You even above other necessary activities. Help me to regularly set aside time to "sit at Your feet"—seeking You, listening to You, and hearing from You.

In Your Name, Amen.

Spiritual Discipline

Exercise in Yielding (The Discipline of Submission)

". . . Train yourself to be godly" (1 Timothy 4:7).

". . . Exercise thyself . . . unto godliness" (1 Timothy 4:7 KJV).

Christ is formed in the disciple as we hear and yield. Faithful disciples participate in this maturing process much like athletes exercise physically.

Gymnasia, the Greek word for "exercise," means "to train oneself." With regard to yielding, several opportunities for training have been made available to us. These disciplines of submission train us to deny ourselves, develop trust, and discern the ways of God.

Review the avenues of submission noted below. Pause and meditate on the Scriptures related to each one, listening for the Holy Spirit's prompting:

SUBMISSION TO GOD
"Submit yourselves, then, to God . . ." (James 4:7).

SUBMISSION TO HUMAN AUTHORITIES
"Everyone must submit himself to the governing authorities, for there is no authority except that which God has established. The authorities that exist have been established by God" (Romans 13:1).

"Submit yourselves for the Lord's sake to every human institution, whether to a king as the one in authority, or to governors as sent by him for the punishment of evildoers and the praise of those who do right. For such is the will of God that by doing right you may silence the ignorance of foolish men" (1 Peter 2:13–15 NASB).

"Servants, be submissive to your masters with all respect, not only to those who are good and gentle, but also to those who are unreasonable. For this finds favor, if for the sake of conscience toward God a person bears up under sorrows when suffering unjustly" (vv. 18, 19 NASB).

SUBMISSION WITHIN FAMILY RELATIONSHIPS

"Then [Jesus] went down to Nazareth with [Mary and Joseph] and was obedient to them . . ." (Luke 2:51).

"Husbands, love your wives, just as Christ loved the church and gave himself up for her" (Ephesians 5:25).

"Wives, submit to your husbands as to the Lord" (v. 22).

"Children, obey your parents in the Lord, for this is right" (6:1).

SUBMISSION WITHIN THE CHURCH

"Submit to one another out of reverence for Christ" (Ephesians 5:21).

"Obey your leaders and submit to them, for they keep watch over your souls as those who will give an account. Let them do this with joy and not with grief, for this would be unprofitable for you" (Hebrews 13:17 NASB).

". . . Clothe yourselves with humility toward one another . . ." (1 Peter 5:5 NASB).

Personal Reflection:

In order to additionally "exercise" my heart in yielding, it may be helpful to give attention to submission in the following areas or relationships: _____

_____

Prayerful Reflection:

Lord Jesus, my desire is to live a life submitted to You, committed to yield even before I have heard all that You desire of me. In order to deepen and quicken my inclination to yield, I sense it is important that I exercise additional submission in this area or relationship:

_____

_____

By Your Spirit, enable me to submit willingly and joyfully, knowing that it is for my good.

In Your name, Amen.

Scripture Memory

John 4:34

"'My food,' said Jesus, 'is to do the will of him who sent me and to finish his work.'"

Chapter 4

Transformed by Experiencing Scripture

"Your word is a lamp to my feet and a light for my path" (Psalm 119:105).

The last week of November has, for several years, found me joining ministry leaders from around the United States for two days of golf, usually in Florida. This golf retreat is a special time of fellowship and networking for what many would call "celebrity" pastors and church leaders. Fifty or so famous leaders with huge churches, denominational responsibilities, TV and radio ministries, publishing contracts, and the like, gather among peers away from the maddening crowds.

Why I would be among them? As I am neither famous nor a great golfer, the question is reasonable. My role is primarily to be a confidant and counselor, something of a golf chaplain. The event's host, Jay, has at times scheduled me in a foursome with leaders who are dealing with troubled marriages, kids, and churches, or with tragedies, health traumas, and temptations. As we make our way through two days of golf, meals, and fellowship times, I consider it a privilege to provide a little care and comfort. It fits well with our ministry's calling to serve the church by helping to restore Great Commandment/Great Commission relevance.

A few years back, Jay called me about a month before the upcoming golf retreat to discuss the assignment of the foursomes. He affirmed my usual request to play Monday with my friend Roger, a mega-church pastor from Arizona, and he told me that we would be joined by two hurting pastors—one with a troubled marriage and one whose grandchild had been killed in a tragic accident. As I made notes, wanting to remember these leaders in prayer, Jay moved on to the second day's plans: "On Tuesday I've put you in a foursome with . . . " He then named three famous leaders. "Why those three?" I wondered. "Because I think it could help your ministry," Jay said.

Jay's heart is always to serve and support, but his words stirred in me thoughts like, "I didn't know our ministry needed help!" and "I'm always excited to see what God does in a new relationships, but anything that approximates the world's way of 'mutual self-promotion' is something to be avoided." After I awkwardly expressed a mixture of gratitude and uneasiness, we concluded the phone conversation.

The golf retreat soon arrived. Monday's round went well from a relational standpoint, if not on my scorecard. I was able to minister to the two hurting pastors, and was nourished by fellowship with my friend Roger. During our Monday evening fellowship time, some discussed golf, while others talked of more eternal things. Standing with several others discussing a Garden Tomb project in Israel, I overheard behind me a conversation that would change the rest of my evening. A voice I recognized inquired, "Who are you playing with tomorrow?" Another voice I recognized replied, "It looks like I have to play with Ferguson." Obviously, one of the famous pastors I was to play with on Tuesday was less than excited! The words hurt; the rejection was real.

The rest of the evening was a blur of self-doubt, hurt, and anger. My dread of the next day was almost overwhelming. Darkness had overtaken my soul. I prayed, trying to take some thoughts captive. By the session's conclusion, I had become emotionally numb. But in the parting social interactions, Roger let me know that he knew what I had overheard. His sensitivity and affirmation ministered to my heart more than he knew.

Riding an elevator alone to my room, there was a special sense of God being ". . . the God of all comfort" (2 Corinthians 1:3). As I turned the key to unlock my door, reassuring Scriptures hidden in my heart flooded my soul: "Therefore, there is now no condemnation for those who are in Christ Jesus" (Romans 8:1)*; ". . . If God is for us, who can be against us?" (v. 31); ". . . Where the Spirit of the Lord is, there is freedom" (2 Corinthians 3:17); "Do not repay evil with evil or insult with insult, but with blessing . . ." (1 Peter 3:9).

As I went into my room, my spirit was not as heavy. Almost without thinking, I picked up the phone and asked the operator for the room of the pastor who was less than pleased to be playing with me the next day. Knowing that he was likely still downstairs, I felt fairly certain I would only get his room voice mail. I wanted to repay insult with blessing, relying on the Spirit of Christ to bring freedom.

> **It is humanity's way to strive for mutual self-promotion. Whatever "help" our ministry needed, Jehovah Jireh would provide. God was protecting me from the ways of this world.**

"Brother _____," I said, "this is David Ferguson. You, no doubt, come to these events anticipating fellowship with those you've not seen in a while, as do I. If it's okay with you, I'd like to play with Pastor Roger again tomorrow and give you the opportunity to play with someone you've not seen recently. Bless you. Good night."

Sensing a measure of release and the Lord's presence, I sat down on the bed, only to be confronted by this question from the Lord: "David, why did I let you overhear those comments?" Rationally, I considered the options: God did not have to let me hear those hurtful words in the first place, and I knew He did not let me hear them just to hurt me. Then came His quiet, still prompting: "David, I protected you—for My thoughts are not your thoughts, and My ways are not your ways."

The living truth of Isaiah 55:8, hidden away in my heart, brought deep reassurance to my soul. It is humanity's way to strive for mutual self-promotion. Whatever "help" our ministry needed, Jehovah Jireh would provide. God was protecting me from the ways of this world. My hurt turned to gratitude; my pain was replaced by wonder that God's Word had come alive, leading me ". . . out of darkness into His wonderful light" (1 Peter 2:9). Feelings of self-doubt and rejection had overtaken me, but Isaiah 55:8 was the light that I needed to walk out of the darkness.

> **"Walk while you have the light, lest the darkness overtake you" (John 12:35 RSV). This verse suggests that all we have to do for the darkness of temptation, compromise, sin, and self to overtake us is to stop walking!**

Jesus admonished His disciples to "Walk while you have the light, lest the darkness overtake you" (John 12:35 RSV). This verse suggests that all we have to do for the darkness of temptation, compromise, sin, and self to overtake us is to stop walking! The Father lovingly reveals "light" from His Word, so that faithful disciples might walk in it, hearing and yielding with hearts longing to please Him.

An Experience With God's People

"I will delight in your principles and not forget your word" (Psalm 119:16 NLT).

Disciples delight in God's Word, not forgetting how His truth has blessed them. Consider a specific Bible verse that has become especially meaningful to you. Then reflect on how God made it alive for you, leading you out of darkness into light.

Maybe God used a particular Bible verse (like John 3:16) to draw you out of sin's darkness into a new-birth encounter with Christ.

Maybe God used a particular Bible promise (like Psalm 23) to lead you out of a valley of despair into "green pastures."

Maybe God used a specific Bible admonition (like Ephesians 4:31) to challenge you to rid yourself of some area of darkness so that you could walk with Him and hear His voice.

I'm grateful to God for using _____ *in my life in order to lead me out of the*
(Scripture passage)

darkness of _____ *and into the light of* _____.

After sharing your responses with your partner or small group, pray together, expressing gratitude for the power, promise, and potential of the light of God's Word.

NOURISHED BY THE LIGHT OF THE WORD

"Like newborn babes, long for the pure milk of the word, so that by it you may grow . . ."
(1 Peter 2:2 NASB).

Disciples grow in maturity as they are nourished by the Word of God. Satan sought to tempt Christ in the desert, but Christ overcame Him by continuing to walk in the light of the Word of God (Matthew 4:1–11). His declarations speak to the power and necessity of being nourished by the Word: "'Man shall not live on bread alone, but on every word that comes from the mouth of God'" (v. 4). As we live out the divine calling to express and extend God's presence in a dark world, we must take full advantage of every opportunity to encounter God in His Word and to experience its nourishing benefits and blessings.

- As we **hear** the Word taught, preached, and shared, our faith will be strengthened: "Faith comes from hearing the message . . ." (Romans 10:17).

- As we **read** the Word, we will be blessed: "Blessed is the one who reads the words of this prophecy . . ." (Revelation 1:3).

- As we **study** the Word, we will be approved by God as ". . . a workman who . . . correctly handles the word of truth" (2 Timothy 2:15).

- As we **memorize** the Word, we will be less vulnerable to sin: "I have hidden your word in my heart that I might not sin against you" (Psalm 119:11).

- As we **meditate** upon the Word, our yielding to it will increase: "Do not let this Book of the Law depart from your mouth; meditate on it day and night, so that you may be careful to do everything written in it . . ." (Joshua 1:8). Meditation upon the Word will also produce spiritual prosperity, health, and fruitfulness (Psalm 1:1–3).

Pause and Reflect

How many of these five ways of being nourished by the Word of God have you taken advantage of this past week?

Sadly, too many of God's children remain "babes," as week by week they come to hear God's Word preached or taught by others, but rarely take advantage of other avenues of nourishment.

What other ways of "feeding upon" the Word might you desire to pursue at this time? How might you go about it?

I could pursue more of these additional ways of being nourished by God's Word (circle any that apply):

Hearing   Reading   Studying   Memorizing   Meditating

by _____

_____.

(For example: Memorizing—*by memorizing the Scripture passages for each chapter in* Relational Discipleship.

Reading—*by following a Daily Bible Reading plan in order to read my Bible every day.*

Studying—*by completing the Follow-up Bible Studies in* Relational Discipleship *and discussing them with my small group or mentor.*)

THE LIGHT OF SCRIPTURE FOR DOCTRINE AND BEHAVIOR

"All Scripture is God-breathed and is useful for teaching, rebuking, correcting and training in righteousness" (2 Timothy 3:16).

Paul's words to Timothy reveal four important functions, which Scripture performs in the life of the true disciple: it serves to teach, to rebuke, to correct, and to train. We will consider the first three of these functions as we examine Scripture's revelation concerning right doctrine and right behavior.

Teaching Right Doctrine—The Rational Purpose of Scripture

One significant purpose of God's Word is to **teach** us what we should believe. The darkness of human philosophies and belief systems is pierced by the light of Scripture:

- The darkness of universalism claims there are many gods, all of which give equal access to eternal life. But the light of Scripture declares, "Salvation is found in no one else, for there is no other name under heaven given to men by which we must be saved" (Acts 4:12).

> **One significant purpose of God's Word is to teach us what we should believe.**

- The darkness of humanism, which places man at the center of all things, is exposed as error by the light of Scripture's first four words: "In the beginning God . . . " (Genesis 1:1).

- The darkness of materialism is exposed as a lie to disciples who walk in the light of Christ's warning: "'What good is it for a man to gain the whole world, yet forfeit his soul'"(Mark 8:36)?

Faithful disciples long to receive right doctrine as they hear, read, study, memorize, and meditate on God's Word.

Pause and Reflect

What scriptural truth has impacted what you believe?

An important Bible truth that has shaped what I believe is found in _____.
This passage has helped me to believe that _____.

(For example: *An important Bible truth that has shaped what I believe is found in James 1:2–4. This passage has helped me to believe that God is doing good things in me as I choose to persevere through my struggles and pain.*)

Without embracing this truth, I would be overtaken by the darkness of _____.

(For example: *Without embracing this truth, I would be overtaken by the darkness of doubting God's goodness and love.*)

Rebuking and Correcting—The Behavioral Purpose of Scripture

A second valuable purpose of God's Word is to reveal to us how we should live. Scripture has been given to **rebuke** (confront what is wrong) and **correct** (define what is right and equip us to do it). The rebukes of Scripture help us to identify areas of darkness, while the corrections of Scripture point us toward the light.

> A second valuable purpose of God's Word is to reveal to us how we should live. Scripture has been given to rebuke (confront what is wrong) and correct (define what is right and equip us to do it).

- The darkness of man's **selfishness and immorality** is rebuked by Scripture:

"The acts of the sinful nature are obvious: sexual immorality, impurity and debauchery; idolatry and witchcraft; hatred, discord, jealousy, fits of rage, selfish ambition, dissensions, factions and envy; drunkenness, orgies, and the like. I warn you, as I did before, that those who live like this will not inherit the kingdom of God" (Galatians 5:19–21).

Scripture then provides correction as it reveals God's light:

"But the fruit of the Spirit is love, joy, peace, patience, kindness, goodness, faithfulness, gentleness and self-control. Against such things there is no law" (vv. 22, 23).

- The darkness of **harsh, critical words** is rebuked by Scripture:

"Let no unwholesome word proceed from your mouth . . . "

Correction is then provided as Scripture guides the disciple into God's light:

". . . but only such a word as is good for edification according to the need of the moment, so that it will give grace to those who hear" (Ephesians 4:29 NASB).

Faithful disciples long to receive from Scripture both reproof and correction for right living as they hear, read, study, memorize, and meditate on the Word.

Pause and Reflect

An important Bible truth that God used to confront what was wrong in my life was

_____

_____.

(For example: *An important Bible truth that God used to confront what was wrong in my life was Matthew 5:37—"Let your 'Yes' be 'Yes,' and your 'No,' 'No.'" This verse showed me that I need to promise less and then do what I promise.*)

An important Bible truth that God used to define what was right and equip me to do it was _____

_____.

(For example: *An important Bible truth that God used to define what was right and equip me to do it was 1 John 1:9 —"If we confess our sins, he is faithful and just and will forgive us our sins and purify us from all unrighteousness." This verse showed me that I need to admit to God when I am wrong so I can experience His forgiveness.*)

An Experience With God's Word

"I am overwhelmed continually with a desire for your laws" (Psalm 119:20 NLT).

Read together the psalmist's declarations and requests in Psalm 119:11–20 (NLT). Reflect on each Scripture, listening for the Holy Spirit's prompting and listen for a specific declaration that you would like to become true for you.

- "I have hidden your word in my heart . . ." (v. 11).
- "I have recited aloud all the laws you have given us" (v. 13).
- "I have rejoiced in your decrees as much as in riches" (v. 14).
- "I will study your commandments and reflect on your ways" (v. 15).
- "I will delight in your principles and not forget your word" (v. 16).
- ". . . I need the guidance of your commands . . ." (v. 19).
- "I am overwhelmed continually with a desire for your laws" (v. 20).

Allow the Lord to impress your heart to become like the psalmist in one of these declarations:

Lord, I sense that You might want me to experience more of the truth of verse _____ *; I want to become someone who* _____.

(For example: *Lord, I sense that You might want me to experience more of the truth of verse 11; I want to become someone who has hidden Your Word in my heart by memorizing it.*)

Share your response with your partner or small group, requesting prayer for yourself that God would make it so.

Then pray, expressing the same requests as the psalmist: ". . . Teach me your principles" (v. 12); "Open my eyes to see the wonderful truths in your law" (v. 18).

THE LIGHT OF SCRIPTURE FOR LOVING RELATIONSHIPS

Training in Righteousness—The Relational Purpose of Scripture

In this closing section, we will explore a third important purpose of God's Word—its relational purpose. In many ways, this is the most significant source of nourishment that the Word offers the believer, yet it is also the one that is most often missing from our scriptural "diet."

In order to understand this relational purpose, we must consider the fourth function of Scripture that Paul mentions to Timothy in 2 Timothy 3:16—that of training us in righteousness, or, more literally, "parenting" us. Derived from the Greek word for "children" (*padeia*), the word "training" (*paideian*) suggests being raised into spiritual maturity by Scripture, in a manner similar to being raised by a loving family into physical and emotional maturity.

> **Jesus said that Scripture ("the law and the prophets") hangs, or depends, upon two commandments: Love God, and love others (Matthew 22:35–40). Scripture has a relational purpose: to lead us into maturity through deepened love relationships with the God who breathed it and with those He loves.**

Scripture has given us the boundaries of right doctrine and right behavior, much like parents give boundaries to their children. But do such boundaries and guidelines—the rules, the "thou shalt nots"—actually raise or mature us? Absolutely not. What brings us to maturity are the loving relationships that exist within the boundaries. A family can have abundant and appropriate rules, restrictions, and guidelines, but if it lacks love-filled relationships, maturity is hindered. So also it is with our approach to Scripture. Scripture is God-breathed, living, and active, and intended to be experienced in loving relationship with the One who wrote it!

Jesus said that Scripture ("the law and the prophets") hangs, or depends, upon two commandments: Love God, and love others (Matthew 22:35–40). Scripture has a relational purpose: to lead us into maturity through deepened love relationships with the God who breathed it and with those He loves. As the Holy Spirit brings revelation concerning this relational purpose, Scripture will seem to "come alive," spurring us to love others, to realize that we are loved, and, above all, to love the One who has given the Word to us.

Scripture Coming Alive With Love Toward Others

Soon after becoming a Christian at the age of 21, I began to be challenged to express God's presence in every area of my life. I was working in a state government office at the time, and my exuberance to pass on my newly found faith frequently found its way into discussions with my co-workers. A drastic re-ordering of my priorities and lifestyle was underway, and it was noticed by those around me.

One who observed the Lord's work in me was Betty, an administrative assistant who had recently been transferred into my area of responsibility. She interrupted my daily office routine on one occasion, tearfully sharing the pain of family troubles. Almost in mid-sentence, her painful sharing turned into a question: "Your life seems to have been radically changed by Christ; what do I need to do?"

In the previous few days of Scripture reading, I had come across an almost identical question in Acts 16:30: "'. . . What must I do to be saved?'" the Philippian jailer inquired of the apostle Paul. I began sharing with Betty along the lines of the apostle Paul's response to the jailer: "Believe in the Lord Jesus, and you will be saved." Then my sharing was interrupted. I paused, speechless, as the rest of Acts 16:31 crossed my mind and heart: "'. . . you and your household.'"

Stumbling over my words, I blurted out, "Betty, maybe we need to wait and share with your husband also so you can both . . . " Before I could finish the thought, Betty interrupted with more tears: "Could we? Would you?"

Both Betty and her husband received Christ as their Savior during the next week. During one of our times of rejoicing together, I heard from her husband these words: "Coming to Christ together as a couple is allowing us to begin again in our relationship. If Betty had come to Christ before me, I'm afraid my pride would have kept me from trusting Him."

God knew that Betty and her husband needed to trust Christ. But He also knew the importance of giving them the opportunity to experience salvation together. Thus, His Spirit had guided me by His Word, making it "come alive" in my heart, so that His love might be expressed toward Betty **and** her husband.

Pause and Reflect

Consider how Scripture has "come alive" in your own life as the Spirit has guided you to better express God's love to others. Recall a time when a specific Bible passage helped you to better live out His love toward someone else. Perhaps, for example . . .

- as a husband, you were guided by the Holy Spirit to 1 Peter 3:7, which called you to ". . . live with your [wife] in an understanding way . . ." (NASB).

- as a wife, you were challenged by 1 Peter 3:4 to express a more ". . . gentle and quiet spirit. . . ."

- as a parent, you were reminded by the Holy Spirit of the admonition of Ephesians 6:4: ". . . Do not provoke your children to anger . . ." (NASB).

- as a Christian, you were prompted by the Holy Spirit to reflect on Ephesians 4:29: "Do not let any unwholesome talk come out of your mouth . . ." thus changing the way you converse with those in your workplace, community, or church.

Complete the following sentence:

I recall when _____ *seemed to come alive in a fresh way, as I was*
                  (Scripture passage)

challenged to _____

_____.

Scripture Coming Alive With Love Toward You

We live in a world of tribulation (John 16:33 KJV), vulnerable to Satan's attacks and the inevitable pain of life in a fallen world. Knowing this, our heavenly Father will, at times, bring Scripture alive as a fresh testimony of His love toward us.

An encounter with my friend Pastor Roger a few years back left me feeling uncertain and inadequate. During a visit to his church in Tucson, we were discussing various sermon series we were making available for free download on our website, **www.greatcommandment.net.** Several of my message series were already available, and we wanted to add some of the Great Commandment sermons that Roger had shared with his congregation.

> **Knowing that we live in a world of tribulation (John 16:33 KJV), vulnerable to Satan's attacks and the inevitable pain of life in a fallen world, our heavenly Father will at times bring Scripture alive as a fresh testimony of His love toward us.**

At one point, Roger, somewhat timidly, said, "David, your messages aren't really sermons—they are teaching series." He went on to explain that the messages recorded and transcribed from my conference speaking were different from his weekly sermons because he always had to assume that many hearing the current week's message were not in attendance the previous week. I, on the other hand, was able to base my series of messages on the assumption that my conference attendees remained the same.

Even though his logic had merit, the words, "Yours aren't really sermons" stung, leaving a knot in my stomach. We had advertised my messages as "sermons," and several thousand had been downloaded as "sermons." Had we led people astray?

My heart fought off tinges of rejection, irritation, and disappointment long enough to finish the conversation with Roger, and I soon left for the airport. But while I was still in the church parking lot, my spirit down and my heart flooded by mixed emotions, a particular Bible verse jumped into my head: "It was he who gave some to be apostles, some to be prophets, some to be evangelists, and some to be pastors and **teachers**" (Ephesians 4:11). The Spirit seemed to emphasize the word "teacher," as if to say to me, "David, you're a teacher!" My heart was filled with joy. God had just caused His Word to "come alive" so that I might experience His love for me!

Pause and Reflect

"For everything that was written in the past was written to teach us, so that through endurance and the encouragement of the Scriptures we might have hope" (Romans 15:4).

Consider now a time when the Spirit seemed to bring Scripture alive in order to demonstrate God's love for you in a fresh way. Perhaps, for example . . .

- during a time of discouragement, the Holy Spirit made alive God's promise ". . . that he who began a good work in you will carry it on to completion . . ." (Philippians 1:6).

- during a time of loneliness, Jesus gently reminded you, "'. . . Surely I am with you always, to the very end of the age'" (Matthew 28:20).

- during a time of rejection, you were nourished by the thought that, ". . . If God is for us, who can be against us?" (Romans 8:31).

I recall experiencing a time of _____ *during which the Holy Spirit made Scripture "come alive," bringing me encouragement through the truth of*

_____.

Share your response with you partner or small group, giving thanks to God that, through His Spirit, He kept the promise of Romans 15:4.

Scripture Coming Alive With Love Toward the One Who Wrote It

The Bible is a book of doctrine and teaching, but it is more. It is a book of promises and divine plans, but it is more. It is God's revelation of Himself: His identity, His heart, His hope.

Deep-rooted love for God develops in the disciple's heart as the wonder of His grace and the privilege of serving Him are made real again and again through encountering Him in Scripture. His Spirit reveals to us the One who wrote the Word, empowering us to respond with yielding love.

For example, you might encounter God through His Word as you study the Ten Commandments (Exodus 20) and consider the question, "Why did God give us these instructions?" Of course, the Ten Commandments provide us with doctrine concerning holiness and exhortations for righteous living, but how do they encourage a loving relationship with God? What is their **relational** purpose?

In response to this question, the Spirit might lead you to Deuteronomy 10:13: ". . . Observe the Lord's commands and decrees that I am giving you today for your own good." Joy fills your spirit as you realize that the Father warns us with His "Thou shalt nots" for our own good.

> **Deep-rooted love for God develops in the disciple's heart as the wonder of His grace and the privilege of serving Him are made real again and again through encountering Him in Scripture.**

He loves us and does not want to see us harmed. Your heart is warmed by this reassuring encounter. God's Word has come alive through your study of the Ten Commandments, and you have been touched by God's love. True to the Great Commandment, you are drawn to love Him with all your heart, mind, soul, and strength.

Or perhaps you are preparing a lesson on Christ's sufferings and are drawn to His Gethsemane prayer: "'My soul is overwhelmed with sorrow to the point of death. Stay here and keep watch with me'" (Matthew 26:38). You sense the pain that Christ feels, and your spirit is filled with empathy for this One acquainted with sorrow and grief.

> **The Father warns us with His "Thou shalt nots" for our own good. He loves us and does not want to see us harmed.**

You read on, reaching the point in the narrative where Jesus returns to find the disciples sleeping. Your eyes fill with tears as you read His next words: "'Could you men not keep watch with me for one hour?'" (v. 40). The question seems filled with disappointment and sorrow. Your heart burns with compassion—you experience fellowship with Christ by sharing in His sufferings (Philippians 3:10). His Word is alive!

Maturing disciples walk in the light of God's Word, protected by the boundaries of right doctrine and right living, and nourished by fresh encounters with Him. Thus, at the end of each day, we might reflect not on "What did I get done today?" but rather, "How have I been nourished by Scripture today? What Scriptures have I experienced?"

> **When we meditate, we are developing mental, emotional, and spiritual images of scriptural truth and hiding them away in our hearts. These images are then available for the Holy Spirit to rekindle as He leads us out of darkness into His marvelous light.**

One means of experiencing Scripture in a transforming way is through the discipline of meditation. When we meditate, we are developing mental, emotional, and spiritual images of scriptural truth and hiding them away in our hearts. These images are then available for the Holy Spirit to rekindle as He leads us out of darkness into His marvelous light. As we close this chapter, take time to experience the following meditation as an example of this process.

An Experience With God's Son

"Who will bring any charge against those whom God has chosen? It is God who justifies. Who is he that condemns? Christ Jesus, who died—more than that, who was raised to life—is at the right hand of God and is also interceding for us" (Romans 8:33, 34).

Picture yourself walking into a courtroom—an intimidating place for most of us. As you enter—alone, uncertain of why you are even there—your anxiety is real. As you move further into the room, you begin to notice the faces of those who have accused you. Perhaps they are acquaintances who have criticized or judged you. Maybe they are people from your past who rejected, neglected, or abused you. Perhaps they are those whose love and acceptance was always contingent on your performance. Your anxiety turns to fear, your self-doubt to self-condemnation. You are alone with your accusers.

Now imagine that into the courtroom walks Jesus Christ. He does not take a place behind the courtroom bench as a judge (though He has every right to), but instead walks right up beside you. He puts His arm around you and gently bows with you to your knees.

Kneeling beside you is the only One who has the right to bring any charge against you. But as you listen to His soft words, you realize that He is not accusing you—He is interceding for you! He is praying for the burdens of your heart—requesting provision, speaking blessing over your relationships, and most importantly, asking that you might experience freedom from condemnation.

During a moment of stillness, you hear Jesus ask, "Where are your accusers?" You lift your eyes and realize that the courtroom is empty. Those who had criticized and judged you, rejected and neglected you, are all gone. Your anxiety has turned to joy; your fear has become peace. Then you hear Jesus say, "'. . . Neither do I condemn you . . .'" (John 8:11).

No wonder Paul writes, "Therefore, there is now no condemnation for those who are in Christ Jesus, because through Christ Jesus the law of the Spirit of life set me free . . ." (Romans 8:1, 2).

The only One who has the right to judge you is praying for you! Meditate quietly on this wondrous truth. Then offer a prayer of thanksgiving, praise, and worship with your partner or small group.

Jesus declared, "'I am the light of the world. Whoever follows me will never walk in darkness, but will have the light of life'" (John 8:12). In Chapter 5, we will explore the second source of God's light: His Son. We will see that God reveals Himself to us as we walk in the light of His Son Jesus, being nourished by our intimacy with Him.

CHAPTER 4 FOLLOW-UP PROJECTS
1. **Bible Doctrine:** The Light of God's Word
2. **Spiritual Discipline:** Living in the Present Free to Hear and Yield to God
3. **Scripture Memory:** Psalm 119:105; 2 Timothy 3:16

Bible Doctrine

The Light of God's Word

The English word *Bible* comes from the Greek word *biblion*, or "book." The Bible is not merely a book, however—it is **the** Book! This study of Bible doctrine will help us understand its purposes more deeply and cultivate in us the desire to encounter God in His Word.

Look up the passages, then fill in the blanks to cement in your mind and heart the truth about The Truth. (The blanks fit the NIV translation, but you can use other translations as well.)

SCRIPTURE COMES TO US FROM GOD; IT IS "GOD'S WORD."

- "All Scripture is_____ - _____ and is _____ for teaching, rebuking, correcting and training in righteousness" (2 Timothy 3:16).

- ". . . Men spoke _____ _____ as they were carried along by the _____ _____" (2 Peter 1:21).

THE BIBLE'S DIVISION INTO OLD AND NEW TESTAMENTS GIVES INSIGHT INTO THE BIBLE'S THEME OF RELATIONSHIP BETWEEN GOD AND MAN.

The word *testament* actually means "covenant" or "agreement." Thus, the Old Testament records the old covenant or agreement between God and man, while the New Testament records the new covenant or agreement between God and man.

The Old Testament, which includes the 39 books from _____ to _____, was referred to by Jesus as the "'. . . _____ and the _____ . . .'" (Matthew 22:40).

- "When Abram was ninety-nine years old, the Lord appeared to him and said, 'I am God Almighty; walk before me and be blameless. I will confirm my _____ between me and you . . .'" (Genesis 17:1, 2).

- The Bible's focus on man's "vertical" relationship with God and his "horizontal" relationship with others is seen frequently in Scripture passages like the Ten Commandments. Notice that the first four commandments define the requirements for man's relationship with _____ (Exodus 20:1–11). The next six commandments spell out guidelines for man's relationship with _____ (vv. 12–17).

- Micah 6:8 is considered by some to be a one-verse summary of the Old Testament: "He has showed you, O man, what is good. And what does the Lord require of you? To act _____ and to love _____ and to walk humbly with _____ _____."

- Old Testament saints entered into covenant with God not by their good works or even by keeping the Law, but by _____ (Hebrews 11:1–40). Their faith was in the biblical promise of a coming Savior who would be "pierced for our _____ . . ." and ". . . crushed for our _____ . . ." (Isaiah 53:5).

This New Covenant in Christ's blood is the subject of **the New Testament,** which contains 27 books, from _____ to _____. The Savior who is promised in the Old Testament is made known in the New Testament, beginning with the angel's announcement to Mary.

- "But the angel said to her, 'Do not be afraid, Mary, you have found favor with God. You will be with child and give birth to a son, and you are to give him the name Jesus. He will be great and will be called the _____ of the _____ _____. The _____ _____ will give him the throne of his father David, and he will reign over the house of Jacob forever; his _____ will never end.'

- 'How will this be,' Mary asked the angel, 'since I am a _____?' The angel answered, 'The _____ _____ will come upon you, and the power of the Most High will overshadow you. So the holy one to be born will be called the _____ of _____'" (Luke 1:30–35).

- This was in direct fulfillment of an Old Testament prophecy given through Isaiah: "'The virgin will be with child and will give birth to a son, and they will call him Immanuel'—which means, '_____ _____ _____'" (Matthew 1:23).

The promised Old Testament Savior had come! Under this New Covenant, we enter into relationship with God by faith—faith that Christ, lived, died, and rose again, taking away the sins of the world.

- "For it is by _____ you have been saved, through _____ —and this not from yourselves, it is the gift of God" (Ephesians 2:8).

In the New Testament, just as in the Old, we see an emphasis on the crucial importance of both "vertical" and "horizontal" relationships:

- "One of the teachers of the law came and heard them debating. Noticing that Jesus had given them a good answer, he asked him, 'Of all the commandments, which is the most important?'

- 'The most important one,' answered Jesus, 'is this: "Hear, O Israel, the Lord our God, the Lord is one. _____ the _____ _____ _____ with all your heart and with all your soul and with all your mind and with all your strength."

- 'The second is this: "_____ your _____ as yourself." There is no commandment greater than these'" (Mark 12:28–31).

Take a moment to give thanks to God for the wonderful gift of His Word!

Spiritual Discipline

Living in the Present
Free to Hear and Yield to God

Jesus Christ is the only One who has ever lived each day in the present. He never woke up regretting anything about yesterday, or went to sleep fearful about tomorrow. He heard His Father's voice and experienced His Father's abundance one moment at a time, unhindered by past remorse or future concerns.

"'The thief comes only to steal and kill and destroy; I have come that they might have life, and have it to the full'" (John 10:10).

What are your first waking thoughts, impressions, and feelings each morning? What are the first stirrings of consciousness? Consider three possibilities:

LIVING IN THE PAST
Regrets from yesterday flood your mind. There were things you wanted to say or do but didn't. There were also things you did not want to say or do but did. You were irritated or angered by things: the car that would not start, the child who did not obey, the spouse who would not help, the pastor who did not pastor, the leader who did not lead, or the government that did not govern.

LIVING IN THE FUTURE
You find yourself feeling anxious and worried over a seemingly endless list of things to do. There always seem to be more obligations and duties in front of you than any one person can perform. You begin each day concerned that you will be tossed about by circumstances, used by people, and probably ignored by those you need. Most sadly, you are hindered from hearing the Creator.

LIVING IN THE PRESENT

Gratefulness stirs in your heart because God has created another day and is allowing you to share it. You rejoice in the day that the Lord has made. You expect His leadership and provision. You confidently hope that He will involve you fully in His purposes. You are filled with awe and wonder that you might serve others around you with love and sensitivity, imparting to them not only the gospel, but your very life. You are free to hear God as you pray and meditate on His Son, as you encounter Him in Scripture, as you receive from others in the body, and as He speaks quietly to you in His still, small voice.

Living in the present is part of Christ's promise of abundant life. Living in the past or future is part of the thief's plan to steal, kill, and destroy (John 10:10). Unfortunately, certain unresolved emotions can keep us stuck in the past or fixated on the future:

Hurt, anger, guilt, and condemnation are tied to past events. To the extent that we have not experienced God's provision for these emotions, we will tend to live in the past.

Fear arises in response to thoughts about what might happen in the future. When fear controls us, we will tend to live in the future.

The graphic below illustrates this principle:

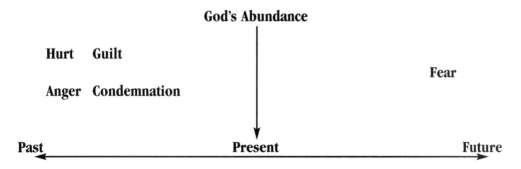

Hearing God requires that the disciple's heart be free from hurt, anger, guilt, condemnation, and fear.

Guilt Needs to Be Confessed First to God . . . (1 John 1:9).
God, it was wrong of me to_____.
Let my heart be saddened by how I have hurt You. Forgive me and change me.

Then to Those We Have Hurt (James 5:16).
It was wrong of me to_____.
Please forgive me.

Anger Needs to Be Released So Forgiveness Can Take Place (Ephesians 4:31, 32).
Heavenly Father, stir my heart with gratitude for how I have been forgiven by You, that I might also forgive others. By Your grace and power, I choose now to forgive _____ for _____
_____. Bring kindness, tenderness, and compassion
to my heart.

Hurt Needs to Be Comforted (Matthew 5:4).
A key to finding freedom from our hurt, sadness, and grief is to first identify it, rather than minimizing or discounting it:

I think I'm disappointed/sad/hurt that _____
_____.

(For example: *I think I'm disappointed that my father was never home; I grew up not knowing him.*)

Underneath my anger, I think I am hurting because _____
_____.

(For example: *Underneath my anger, I think I am hurting because I am not respected at work—my contributions are often not appreciated.*)

I am anxious/fearful at times that I am going to be hurt again, like when _____
_____.

(For example: *I am fearful at times that I am going to be hurt again, like when my best friend at work lied to my boss about me.*)

God's Comfort Needs to Be Received Directly (2 Corinthians 1:3, 4).
Prayerfully reflect on these times of hurt/tragedy/loss, and allow the Holy Spirit to touch your heart with an image of Jesus with tear-filled eyes. The God of all comfort weeps for you, just as He did for His friend, Mary (John 11:35).

God's Comfort Needs to Be Received Through Others (Matthew 5:4).
Vulnerably share your hurt with a loved one or friend, allowing this person the opportunity to hurt with you. You cannot undo past pain, but you do not need to deal with it alone.

I have come to see that I am still hurting about _____,
and I would like to share my pain with you. As I do, I just need you to listen, seek to understand, and maybe share your sadness for me.

When you are called on to comfort another, you will want to respond with gentleness, understanding, and empathy. Offer reassurances of your affection, and, as appropriate, either your silent presence, or tender words such as, "I am so sorry that happened. It hurts me that you were hurt like that because I care for you."

Condemnation Needs to be Overcome by the Gratitude and Freedom That Come Through Truth (Romans 8:1, 2).

I sometimes condemn myself or feel condemnation for _____.

(For example: *I sometimes condemn myself for yelling at my kids.*)

Condemnation from the evil one seeks to equate our worth with our behavior, telling us that we are terrible people or bad Christians because we do not pray enough, do not read our Bibles enough, yell at our kids, and so on.

Allow the Holy Spirit to take these lies captive, and embrace the truth of who the Creator has declared you to be: You are His child, a joint heir with Christ (Romans 8:17). Your worth is determined by your Creator, and He chose to pay the ultimate price through the gift of His Son (5:8).

Pause to allow gratefulness for God's grace to well up inside you. Recall the apostle Paul's grateful words in Romans 7:24, 25: "What a wretched man I am! Who will rescue me from this body of death? Thanks be to God—through Jesus Christ our Lord!" Compose your own love letter, expressing the awe and wonder of God's love toward you.

Thanks be to God for _____

_____

_____

_____

_____

_____.

(For example: *Thanks be to God for the amazing truth that He always accepts me. No matter how bad my behavior has been, He is always willing to give me another chance.*)

Fear Needs to Be Cast Out by God's Perfect Love (1 John 4:18).
Begin by identifying and tracing your fears:

I am sometimes afraid that _____.

(For example: *I am sometimes afraid that I will lose my job.*)

And if that happens, I am afraid that _____.

(For example: *And if that happens, I am afraid that I will not make it financially. I will have to declare bankruptcy.*)

And if that happens, I am afraid that _____.

(For example: *And if that happens, I am afraid that my spouse will be upset, and maybe even leave me.*)

Underneath each fear is a lie from the "'. . . father of lies'" (John 8:44). Embrace a specific truth from God's Word, hide it in your heart, and meditate on it often.

A specific truth that can help cast out my fears is _____
_____
_____.

(Read and reflect on Numbers 14:17, 18; 1 Samuel 15:29; Luke 15:28; Romans 8:37–39; and 2 Peter 3:8, 9.)

Scripture Memory

Psalm 119:105

"Your word is a lamp to my feet and a light for my path."

2 Timothy 3:16

"All Scripture is God-breathed and is useful for teaching, rebuking, correcting and training in righteousness."

Chapter 5

Transformed by Encountering Jesus

D riving out of the airport parking garage, I wondered if it was too late to call Teresa to let her know I was headed home. After an extended trip to several cities for meetings with denominational leaders, I was anxious to see her. Most of the time we travel and minister together; but on this occasion, we had agreed that she could use a few days at home and some time with our grandkids.

I reached for my cell phone, glancing at the clock on the dashboard—it was well after 10:00 p.m. Teresa would definitely be in bed, likely asleep. The call could wait. I felt disappointed; I wanted to hear her voice. I missed her.

I felt a little down. I began to hurry home (admittedly a bit over the speed limit). *Surely traffic would not be too bad at this hour,* I thought. But only a few miles down the freeway, I topped a hill to find all three lanes of traffic at a dead stop.

Cars were exiting onto the service road—should I follow them or remain where I was? Hoping the traffic would clear up beyond the next hill, I trusted my fate to the freeway. Inching forward, I finally came over the hill. As far as I could see were red taillights, frozen in the landscape.

> **A knot formed in my stomach as regret set in. I hit the steering wheel with my fist, then burst out, "I should have known it would be like this!"**

A knot formed in my stomach as regret set in. I hit the steering wheel with my fist, then burst out, "I should have known it would be like this! I should have gotten off onto the service road!" Then, in a fit of frustration, I suddenly shouted at myself, "You never do anything right!"

As I sat in traffic, going nowhere, the self-condemnation I felt was overwhelming. I was shocked by the intensity of the "darkness" that had robbed me of my excitement to get home. I struggled to analyze what was obviously an overreaction. Surely, part of my disappointment was a result of not being able to call Teresa—maybe I was just missing her more than I had realized. But my attempt at dispassionate analysis was shattered by the return of the accusing thought, *You never do anything right!* In that moment, I suddenly recalled a childhood incident in which I had heard those same words from my father.

One Saturday, I was with Dad in the garage as he worked on our car. At one point, he barked out, in slurred words, "Son, bring me a 5/8-inch open-end wrench." My dad was a retired Marine Drill Sergeant—"Son" was his impersonal title for me (a bit like my official "rank"), and barking commands was his way of communicating. The slur in his speech was something I would understand only later in life—it meant Dad had been drinking. Thankfully, God would eventually free him from alcohol and soften his bark. But on this day, both were painfully present.

With a five-year-old's enthusiasm and a desire to please Dad, I made my way to the toolbox, confident that I could read a "5" and an "8." Unfortunately, I didn't know the difference between open-end and box-end wrenches. Proudly, I returned with a 5/8-inch box-end wrench. My father's reaction left no doubt in my young mind that I had somehow made a mistake. He threw the wrench, cursed, and sent me into the house. As I slammed the door behind me, in tears, I remember him saying, "You never do anything right!"

I was startled out of this reverie by the horn of a car behind me on the freeway. Traffic was moving just a little, but I was not. The darkness of sadness and self-condemnation was overcoming me. I needed something other than rational analysis of my feelings and dredged-up memories. I needed to encounter Jesus.

> **That night, as I sat stuck in freeway traffic and plagued by the darkness of condemnation, this image of Jesus, saddened for me, drew me into the freeing light of His compassion.**

I said two words softly under my breath, "Lord, what—" Then, as if saying the word "Lord" had pushed the button on a video projector, a new image filled my mind. It was an image prompted by the events of my last denominational meeting before catching the plane.

Our discussion had focused on a book project and a lesson on Christ's compassion. Our closing reflection dealt with the irony that the easiest Bible verse to remember is about a God who cries for us: "Jesus wept" (John 11:35).

The image that suddenly flashed across my mind as I sat in my car was of Christ with tear-filled eyes. Emotions surrounding that image washed over my heart. Jesus was sad, weeping not just for Mary, but for me! The pain of the accusing, condemning message that I had carried for so long saddened the Lord. That night, as I sat stuck in freeway traffic and plagued by the darkness of condemnation, this image of Jesus, saddened for me, drew me into the freeing light of His compassion.

I have been in several other traffic jams since that night, and have sometimes guessed wrong concerning which way to go. I have also attempted several "some assembly required" household projects with Teresa, only to be frustrated by the fact that she seems to have much more mechanical ability than I do. Before my freeway encounter with the weeping Jesus, these and countless other inadequacies would have brought feelings of self-condemnation, perhaps prompting me to again think, *You never do anything right!* But only rarely since that encounter has my heart been overtaken by the darkness of that accusing message. Christ brought freedom that night, and "'. . . if the Son sets you free, you will be free indeed'" (8:36).

WALKING IN THE LIGHT OF THE SON BRINGS TRANSFORMATION.

Compassion is the most frequently used word in Scripture to describe the heart of Jesus. His compassion is demonstrated not only as He weeps with Mary, but also as He encounters the blind (Matthew 20:34), the hungry (15:32), the ". . . harassed and helpless . . ." (9:36), the masses with their sick (14:14), a widow who had lost her only son (Luke 7:13), and a man with leprosy (Mark 1:41), among many others. Over the years, the Holy Spirit has led me into many freeing encounters with Christ's compassion, just as He did in that traffic jam—but for what purpose?

"It is for freedom that Christ has set us free . . ." (Galatians 5:1). Certainly, experiencing the compassion of Jesus brings freedom *from* some things—freedom from pain, freedom from sorrow, freedom from aloneness—but there is more. We are also given freedom *to*—in my case, freedom to express to others the compassion I have received from Jesus.

117

I have repeatedly been led by the Spirit to encounter a compassionate Jesus. Through these encounters, He has shaped in me a life and calling of compassion. This is a significant aspect of the message He is working to share through me—not exactly what you would expect of someone raised by a Marine Drill Sergeant father, trained initially in the rational world of nuclear physics and computer science, and skilled in competitive debate!

> **The Father's loving plan is that our encounters with Jesus might transform us into His very image. Faithful disciples diligently pursue fresh encounters with Jesus with yielded hearts, confident that such encounters will make them a little more like Him!**

"But we all . . . beholding . . . the glory of the Lord, are being transformed into the same image from glory to glory" (2 Corinthians 3:18 NASB). The Father's loving plan is that our encounters with Jesus might transform us into His very image. Faithful disciples diligently pursue fresh encounters with Jesus with yielded hearts, confident that such encounters will make them a little more like Him!

Pause and Reflect

Transforming Encounters with Jesus

". . . Predestined to be conformed to the likeness of his Son . . . " (Romans 8:29).

Look back over your own faith journey, reflecting on how God's Spirit has revealed Jesus to you. Has He led you to personal encounters with Him? Has He made you a bit more like Jesus through these encounters?

- Have you been awed by the **love** He displayed by dying for you on the Cross? Was gratefulness for His sacrifice part of what drew you to receive Him as your Savior?

- Have you encountered His **forgiveness** and then become more forgiving yourself?

- Have you been touched by His **acceptance** of you and as a result become more accepting?

- Have you been impressed by His **compassion** for children, outcasts, or foreigners? Has He given you a similar burden to care for those on the fringes of society?

Ask Him to reveal by His Spirit fresh insight concerning your past encounters with Jesus.

As I have encountered Christ in His _____ *, it*
has produced in me the desire to be more _____
_____ .

(For example: *As I have encountered Christ in His acceptance of me, it has produced in me the desire to be more accepting of my own children's uniqueness, recognizing that they are not like me.*)

Share your responses with your partner or small group, celebrating with one another each specific journey of transformation. Then pray, giving thanks for the promise that as we behold Christ, we become like Him!

The Insufficiency of Rational Knowledge for Transformation

"'You diligently study the Scriptures because you think that by them you possess eternal life. These are the Scriptures that testify about me, yet you refuse to come to me to have life'" (John 5:39, 40).

Jesus' rebuke of the Pharisees reminds us that walking in the light of Jesus—being transformed by our encounters with Him—means much more than amassing knowledge about Christ or possessing a

> **Our encounters with Jesus in worship, prayer, meditation, and study are intended to bring about in each of us a life-changing, sanctifying transformation into His image and likeness.**

systematic understanding of His life and teachings. The Pharisees pursued and acquired knowledge, even going so far as to memorize the entire body of Hebrew Scripture. Yet they missed God: "'. . . You have never heard his voice nor seen his form, nor does his word dwell in you, for you do not believe the one he sent'" (vv. 37, 38).

In a similar rebuke, James reminds us that rational assent to Scripture is insufficient: "You believe that there is one God. Good! Even the demons believe that—and shudder" (James 2:19). Even Satan knows that Jesus is the sinless Son of God, who suffered a sacrificial death and rose again. But Satan will not yield to such a revelation of Christ—he will not respond relationally.

Our encounters with Jesus in worship, prayer, meditation, and study are intended to bring about in each of us a life-changing, sanctifying transformation into His image and likeness. As this occurs, we better express His glory and His presence.

HOW TO BE TRANSFORMED BY ENCOUNTERING JESUS: LESSONS FROM THE LEPERS

Years ago, while preparing a message on the story of the ten lepers (Luke 17:11–19), God's Spirit impressed upon me in a fresh way the importance of responding relationally to Jesus. In this section, we will illustrate the key responses that move us beyond a rational understanding of Jesus into transforming encounters with Him.

"Now on his way to Jerusalem, Jesus traveled along the border between Samaria and Galilee. As he was going into a village, ten men who had leprosy met him. They stood at a distance and called out in a loud voice, 'Jesus, Master, have pity on us!'" (vv. 11–13).

On that Tuesday morning years ago, as I read this passage in my study, I remember thinking, *Jesus has already healed other lepers, so the word must be getting out—now ten lepers have shown up!* I understood something of the route that Jesus took, being familiar with the geography after a few trips to Israel. I noted that the lepers addressed Him respectfully as "master" or "teacher," that they vulnerably expressed their need for "pity" or "mercy," and that they displayed a measure of faith that Jesus could in some way help (though they were likely unaware of the magnitude of the miracle that would soon occur). My rational understanding of the background of the story thus seemed adequate enough for me to move further in my message preparation.

"When he saw them, he said, 'Go, show yourselves to the priests.' And as they went, they were cleansed" (v. 14).

As I read this verse, I jotted down my first point: "Obey the Bible." Jesus' admonition to "show yourselves to the priests" was clearly in accordance with the purification requirements of Leviticus 14:1–32.

Then the second point of the message came to me: "Exercise faith." The words, "As they went, they were healed," illustrated an essential component of faith: believing before seeing. By acting as if they were healed before they were healed, the ten men received healing!

Many practical applications would certainly have emerged from these two essential points— "obey the Bible" and "exercise faith." But I still remember thinking, *Show me more.* Then I read the next verse, intrigued by the leper who returned to give Jesus glory:

"One of them, when he saw he was healed, came back, praising God in a loud voice. He threw himself at Jesus' feet and thanked him—and he was a Samaritan" (Luke 17:15, 16).

It was then that I realized that there were deeper lessons—relational lessons—to be gleaned from this passage. Let us allow four "lessons from the lepers" to guide us in our efforts to encounter Jesus and to experience transformation into mature Christlikeness.

Lesson #1: Consider Jesus.
". . . Consider Jesus . . ." (Hebrews 3:1 NASB).

The Greek word *katanoéo,* which is translated "consider" in this passage, means "to think about very carefully, to consider closely." The New International Version captures its meaning, rendering Hebrews 3:1, ". . . fix your thoughts on Jesus. . . ."

Beyond even the essential principles of obedience and faith, more significant to the text of Luke 17 than Samaritan traditions or the geography of the road from Galilee to Jerusalem, is a *person*—Jesus. Let us fix our thoughts on Him!

Pause and Reflect

Considering Jesus

"Jesus asked, 'Were not all ten cleansed? Where are the other nine?'" (Luke 17:17).

Pause and allow the Spirit to reveal Jesus—His heart, His disappointment, His sadness.

"'Were not all ten cleansed?'"

It seems clear that Jesus might have hoped to see all ten return to Him with thanksgiving. What do you sense that He might be feeling in this moment? What emotions are behind the words, "'Where are the other nine'"? Ask Him to reveal His heart to you, so that you might encounter Him.

Then complete this sentence:

I sense that Jesus may be experiencing _____
as He asks, "'Were not all ten cleansed? Where are the other nine?'"

(For example: *sadness, disappointment, hurt, or sorrow.*)

As you worship, pray, meditate, and study, intently considering Jesus, expect the Holy Spirit within you to reveal Jesus—His heart, character, emotions, hopes, plans, and burdens. Once this process of consideration and revelation has begun, we must yield by responding relationally to what the Holy Spirit is revealing.

Lesson #2: Respond Relationally to Jesus.
Consider again Christ's words: "'Were not all ten cleansed? Where are the other nine?'"

This is more than just a curious question. Jesus knew where the other nine were, did He not? The One who knows all things knew that they were making their way to the temple to

Jesus' query was not a rational one, but a relational one—"Why have the other nine not returned?"

show themselves to the priests, just as He had instructed them to do. Jesus' query was not a rational one, but a relational one—"Why have the other nine not returned?"

Consider how you previously completed this sentence:

I sense that Jesus may be experiencing _____ *as He asks, "'Were not all ten cleansed? Where are the other nine?'"*

Now consider the next verse:

"'Was no one found to return and give praise to God except this foreigner?'" (v. 18).

Only the Samaritan leper, the foreigner, came back! The implication of the passage is that the other nine must have been Jewish lepers. Listen as His Spirit whispers, "This is yet another occasion when Jesus came to His own people, '. . . but his own did not receive him'" (John 1:11).

An Experience With God's Son

Responding Relationally to Jesus

"He was despised and rejected by men, a man of sorrows, and familiar with suffering . . ." (Isaiah 53:3).

Pause again, and allow the Spirit to move your heart in response to Jesus.

What do you feel in your heart **for** Jesus?

As I consider the sorrowful Savior, missing the appropriate outpouring of gratitude from nine of His own people, my heart is moved with _____ for Him.

Now tell Jesus about what is in your heart. Respond to Him with compassion and care as you would for your most beloved friend.

Jesus, my heart is touched deeply with _____ as I consider Your feelings of _____. It grieves me deeply that _____ _____.

May my sadness for You in some mysterious way bless You with my love.

In Your name, Amen.

Lesson #3: You Are Transformed.
"I want to know Christ and the power of his resurrection and the fellowship of sharing in his sufferings, becoming like him . . . " (Philippians 3:10).

When we encounter God in His Word, something changes. That "something" will not be God, and it will not be His Word—It will be us!

The Holy Spirit has moved our hearts with compassion for Jesus. We have hurt for Him, been saddened for Him, maybe even shed tears for Him. How long has it been since this has happened? Be honest; He already knows. Maybe it has been too long. By His Spirit, the Lord has brought fresh tenderness to your heart as you entered into the ". . . fellowship of sharing in his sufferings . . ." (Philippians 3:10). You fixed your thoughts upon Jesus, your heart was moved with compassion, and you were transformed a bit more into His image.

I still remember the relational encounter I had with Jesus as I studied Luke 17. As tears of compassion for Jesus filled my eyes, I remember thinking, *Jesus often blesses my life with His grace and demonstrates His love to me as He did to these lepers. I do not ever want Him to look around at those of His children who are offering Him praise and thanksgiving and ask, "Where's David?"*

This encounter changed my priorities and life's purpose. Out of my compassion for a sorrowed Savior came a heartfelt determination to not hurt Jesus as He was hurt by those nine Jewish lepers.

> **I do not ever want Him to look around at those of His children who are offering Him praise and thanksgiving and ask, "Where's David?"**

"May our Lord Jesus Christ himself and God our Father, who loved us and by his grace gave us eternal encouragement and good hope, encourage your hearts and strengthen you in every good deed and word" (2 Thessalonians 2:16, 17).

Pause to Pray

How Are You Being Transformed?

Pause to consider your response, and then share it with the Lord in prayer:

Lord Jesus, as You have moved me to hurt for You, saddened by the fact that only one of the ten men you healed returned to give You praise, I have felt challenged to _____
_____
_____.

(For example: *I have felt challenged to prioritize my relationship with Jesus, and to thank and praise Him when He works in my life.*)

Lesson #4: Jesus Is Blessed, Pleased, and Glorified.
"May the God of peace . . . equip you with everything good for doing his will, and may he work in us what is pleasing to him, through Jesus Christ, to whom be glory for ever and ever. Amen" (Hebrews 13:20, 21).

According to Luke, the Samaritan leper "came back, praising God in a loud voice. He threw himself at Jesus' feet and thanked him . . ." (Luke 17:15, 16). Notice that Jesus didn't respond with embarrassment ("Get up from there. Stop giving Me thanks! I do not need that—I am God!"). Instead, He received the man's praise.

Is it not a mysterious wonder that the Creator can receive pleasure from the created? We do not have a Savior who is so distant that He does not notice the praise of His children, or so stoic that He cannot be moved by it. The Holy Son of God received expressions of thanks from this humble Samaritan leper, and referred to him as the one who returned to ". . . give glory . . ." (v. 18 NASB).

Not only does Jesus receive this worship, He rewards the man's yielded heart and life with even more revelation: "'. . . Your faith has made you well'" (v. 19). The other nine might have thought that their obedient trek to the priest caused their healing, but this ex-leper now knew better. His encounter with the Messiah had transformed his life. But more importantly, he experienced the incredible privilege of blessing, pleasing, and glorifying God.

An Experience With God's People

"For from him and through him and to him are all things. To him be the glory forever! Amen" (Romans 11:36).

Pause and consider the riches of God's grace toward you. Maybe you have not been healed of leprosy, but He has given you countless blessings and provisions.

Be still before the Lord. Make your way to your knees. Consider the wonder that His Holy Spirit . . .

- has revealed a saddened Savior.

- has empowered compassion in your heart.

- has reminded you of the privilege of giving Him praise.

- now invites you to bless Him and bring Him glory through your thanksgiving.

Now pray with your partner or small group, blessing Jesus and giving Him glory.

Jesus, my heart is filled with _____ as I consider how You have blessed me in these ways: _____
_____.

I want to bless You, Lord. Thank You for all of Your blessings, but most especially for
_____
_____
_____.

BELIEVING, OBEYING, AND RELATING

". . . We will in all things grow up into him who is the Head, that is, Christ" (Ephesians 4:15).

Maturity, discipleship, and transformation into the likeness of Christ are primarily matters of relating to the One into whose likeness we are growing. Faithful disciples are nourished and transformed by the freshness of their encounters with Jesus, the Head.

If events could sanctify us, Christians in the Western world would surely be among the kingdom's most saintly. If exposure to the Christian message and religious media could produce fully devoted followers of Christ, we would turn the world upside-down for Christ, as did the first century church. If camps, conferences, mission trips, and concerts could instill the faith in the next generation, we would not be struggling to make disciples of our own children.

Sadly, multitudes of Christians have come to think that discipleship is only about being able to claim, "I believe" and "I obey." Let us return to Luke 17 to reinforce the critical nature of relating to Him, fixing our eyes upon Jesus, the author and perfecter of our faith (Hebrews 12:2).

Believing and Obeying: Necessary, but Not Sufficient

Picture the scene in Jerusalem as crowds surround the nine former lepers. The priests have verified the healings and officially restored these nine formerly unclean outcasts to full participation in Jewish society. Family and friends are overwhelmed with excitement at this miraculous turn of events. The nine themselves are still in shock.

Now imagine the conversation that might have occurred between these nine men and the onlookers:

> **Sadly, multitudes of Christians have come to think that discipleship is only about being able to claim, "I believe" and "I obey."**

- Imagine that the nine men were asked, "Do you believe that Jesus can heal people?" They would have most certainly responded, "Sure, we believe."

- Imagine that they were also asked, "What has brought you here to Jerusalem, to the sacred temple?" The men's response would certainly have been, "We did what Jesus instructed us to do and what the Law demands. We obeyed."

This imaginary conversation illustrates a foundational principle for our understanding of our life calling and purpose, and for our pursuit of genuine discipleship and spiritual formation. The nine lepers could have rightly claimed that they believed and obeyed. But while it is certainly essential to believe in the Lord Jesus Christ (John 3:16) and to obey—to ". . . live a life worthy of the calling you have received" (Ephesians 4:1)— in order to fulfill life's ultimate purpose, something else must be added: a loving relationship with the author and perfecter of our faith.

What Else Is Needed: Transforming Relational Encounters With Jesus

Right belief and right behavior, as significant as they are, do not transform us into the likeness of Jesus. Witness the Pharisees: They certainly had belief and behavior down to a science, yet the most cursory examination of the New Testament reveals that they were missing something very important.

Let us return to the Samaritan leper, humbly bowed at the feet of Jesus, giving Him praise. In contrast to the other nine, he demonstrates that following Jesus is fundamentally about developing an intimate relationship with Him.

Relational encounters with Jesus require that beliefs that are grounded in God's written Word come alive by His Spirit through a grateful and yielded relationship with Jesus, the Living Word. In these encounters, we walk in His light, while also boldly shining His light toward others (Matthew 5:14–16).

Great Commandment love—loving Jesus with all our heart, soul, mind, and strength—empowers Great Commission passion to share Him with others. A commitment to right belief and right behavior that is not grounded in this deep love for Christ will never birth the same passion.

A Lifestyle of Longing to Relate to Jesus

Recall Jesus' words of affirmation for His friend, Mary, as she was seated at His feet, listening to His word: "'. . . Mary has chosen what is better, and it will not be taken away from her . . .'" (Luke 10:42). Mary, much like the Samaritan

> **Faithful, maturing followers sit humbly at the feet of Jesus, giving careful, deep consideration to Him. But this lifestyle, though empowered by His Spirit, must be chosen.**

leper, humbly longed to relate to Jesus, the object, author, and perfecter of her faith. Faithful, maturing followers sit humbly at the feet of Jesus, giving careful, deep consideration to Him. But this lifestyle, though empowered by His Spirit, must be chosen. Disciples never "stumble into" maturity and the fulfillment of their life's purpose—the transformational process of encountering Jesus must be chosen, pursued. The psalmist says it like this: "As the deer pants for streams of water, so my soul pants for you, O God. My soul thirsts for God, for the living God. When can I go and meet with God?" (Psalm 42:1, 2).

As this thirst develops in us, we come to view times of worship, meditation, fellowship, prayer, and study of the Word as privileged opportunities to pursue and encounter Jesus. Through these encounters, our relationship with Him deepens and a relational history develops. As in any relationship, touching memories and emotional images are etched on our hearts, ever ready to be recalled and embraced.

For example . . .

- a recent time of worship moved me from singing about "surveying the wondrous cross" to experiencing overwhelming wonder as I heard the Lord whisper to my spirit, "And I did it for you."

- in the acceptance of my loving grandfather, I encountered the outstretched arms of Jesus.

- watching Teresa's loving excitement about our first grandson, I was led to a powerful realization that Jesus is excited to love me.

- times of prayer have led me straight to Him, comforted by the thought that He is already interceding for me.

As a result of many occasions of worship, prayer, study, and meditation, portrayals of Christ are hidden in my heart, revealing Jesus to my soul. Stored away like precious treasures are images of . . .

- the weeping Jesus of John 11:35.

- the saddened, gratitude-deprived Jesus of Luke 17:17, 18.

- the supportive, encouraging Jesus of Luke 22:32.

- the welcoming Jesus of Luke 18:16.

- the accepting Jesus of Luke 19:1–10.

- the interceding Jesus of Romans 8:34.

When the darkness of defeat or despair, sin or self, attack or accusation, comes upon me, my soul, like the psalmist's, goes "panting" after Jesus. I am learning (ever so slowly, it seems) that life's purpose is found in a Person, and that encountering Jesus often and afresh brings transformation into His likeness.

The Motivation to Pursue Jesus

God is longing for us to pursue Him because He delights in revealing more of Himself to us. Whether through worship, prayer, meditation, and study, or through the mundane happenings of everyday life, God is longing to let us in on the divine! This wondrous truth strengthens our motivation to pursue Him.

> **He is longing for us to pursue Him because He delights in revealing more of Himself to us. Whether through worship, prayer, meditation, and study, or through the mundane happenings of everyday life, God is longing to let us in on the divine! This wondrous truth strengthens our motivation to pursue Him.**

Throughout Scripture, we find Christ revealing Himself to others, sometimes when they least expect it. The disciples on the Emmaus Road, for example, thought that they were having a perfectly normal conversation with a fellow traveler (albeit a fellow traveler who seemed to be extraordinarily knowledgeable about Old Testament prophecy). But throughout Jesus' discourse about the Scriptural significance of the Messiah, He was gradually revealing Himself—His wisdom, His nature, His loving concern, and, finally, His identity (Luke 24:13–32).

The Lord also made occasional "special appearances" to His followers in the Old Testament. One such appearance is to Abraham and Sarah in Genesis 18. After spending a day with Abraham and his family, during which He affirmed that they would miraculously give birth within a year, the Lord prepared to depart. Then He paused, asking Himself, "'Shall I hide from Abraham what I am about to do?'" (v. 17). Like a good friend, the Lord halted in the midst of His divine agenda to consider Abraham. He stopped to let Abraham in on what He was about to do. What if He is longing to do the same for you?

Imagine living as if God, by His Spirit, might pay you a visit at any time, at any place, in any circumstance. Envision yourself approaching times of worship, prayer, Bible study, and fellowship with an eager expectation of His visitation. What if God's heart is to let us in on what He is up to? Might our motivation to pursue Him increase if we truly believed that He longs to reveal Himself to us?

An Experience With God's Word

"'I no longer call you servants, because a servant does not know his master's business. Instead, I have called you friends, for everything that I learned from my Father I have made known to you'" (John 15:15).

Jesus desires a deeper relationship with you, desires to reveal to you what He has learned from the Father. Just as God longed to reveal to Abraham what He was about to do, He also longs to relate to us intimately, as friends. You have chosen to pursue Him, only to find that He is also pursuing you!

Pause to consider that He wants to reveal to you His heart, His ways. What does that do to your heart? If you were to embrace this truth, would you, like Abraham and the Samaritan leper, run and bow before Him? Would you, like Mary, choose to listen at His feet?

Complete these sentences:

Lord Jesus, as I embrace the wonder of friendship with You and consider Your longing for intimacy between You and me, my heart is moved with _____.

I am motivated to pursue You more intimately through _____
_____
_____.

(For example: *regular devotional reading of the Bible; listening as well as talking to You in prayer; regularly asking You to reveal Yourself to me, especially when I am having a hard time; investing time in really "considering" You as I read about You in the Gospels; meditating on You in my mind and heart as I worship.*)

Share your responses with your partner or small group. Then pray together, expressing your desire to pursue an intimate relationship with Jesus, walking in His light in order to behold Him and be transformed.

In Chapter 6, we will explore the third source of divine light: God's people. We will find that our lives are greatly enriched and transformed as we experience genuine fellowship with other believers.

CHAPTER 5 FOLLOW-UP PROJECTS
1. **Bible Doctrine:** The Light of God's Son
2. **Ministry Skill:** Sharing Your Faith in Christ With Others
3. **Scripture Memory:** 2 Corinthians 3:18 NASB

Bible Doctrine

The Light of God's Son

Instructions: Read through the following study, looking up the passages and filling in the blanks as a way of emphasizing key truths. Then respond to the experiential exercise at the end of the study.

"'. . . Let **us** make man in **our** image . . .'" (Genesis 1:26, emphasis added).

With these words from the opening chapter of Scripture, we are introduced to the divine mystery of the Trinity. The one and only true God exists in three persons, each of whom is recognized by Scripture as God:

- The _____ is recognized as God (John 6:27; 1 Peter 1:2).

- _____ _____ is recognized as God (Titus 2:13).

- The _____ _____ is recognized as God (Acts 5:3, 4).

However, even though these three exist as One, Scripture compels us to also know them as distinct persons:

- Jesus distinguishes the _____ from Himself (John 5:37).

- Jesus distinguishes the _____ _____ from Himself and from the Father (John 14:16, 17).

In this study, we will specifically explore foundational truths concerning Jesus, the second Person of the Trinity.

KNOWING CHRIST, THE SECOND PERSON OF THE TRINITY

Christ Has Always Existed.

Scripture speaks of Christ (or "the Word") existing eternally:

- "In the _____ was the Word . . ." (John 1:1).

- "He is _____ all things . . ." (Colossians 1:17).

- "". . . _____ Abraham was born, I _____ . . ."" (John 8:58).

Christ Appeared to People Before He Was Born as a Man.

Many of these appearances are recorded in the Old Testament. "The glory of the Lord" and "the Word of the Lord" are Old Testament names that can reasonably be associated with Christ, the second Person of the Trinity. Additionally, the names, "the Angel of the Lord" or simply "the Lord," are sometimes used to indicate such an appearance.

The people to whom the Lord appeared include (but are not limited to) . . .

- Hagar (Genesis 16:7–13).
- Abraham (Genesis 22:11–15).
- Balaam (Numbers 22:21–35).
- Gideon (Judges 6:11–40).
- Samson's mother (Judges 13:2–5).
- Samuel (1 Samuel 15:10, 11).
- Solomon (1 Kings 6:11–13).
- Isaiah (2 Kings 20:4–6).

Note that often the person begins by interacting with "the Word of the Lord" or "the angel of the Lord" and then the text shifts to simply, "the Lord." Genesis 18:1–33, by contrast, is an example of an appearance of the eternal, pre-incarnate Christ in which He is referred to throughout as "the Lord":

- "The Lord appeared to Abraham . . ." (v. 1).

- "Then the Lord said . . . " (vv. 10, 13, 17, 20).

Old Testament "Pictures" of Christ Are Fulfilled by Him in the New Testament.

Three particular Old Testament pictures of Christ (and their corresponding New Testament fulfillments) deserve special mention:

- The Passover Lamb (Exodus 12:21–28): "'Look, the _____ of God, who takes away the sin of the world'" (John 1:29).

- The Obedient Sacrifice (Psalm 40:6–8): "Then I said, 'Here I am . . . I have come to do your will, O God'" (Hebrews 10:7).

- The Beloved _____ (Psalm 2:7): "'You are My beloved _____ . . .'" (Mark 1:11 NASB).

The Incarnation of Christ: The Second Person of the Trinity Became a Man.

- "In the beginning was the _____, and the _____ was with God, and the _____ was God" (John 1:1).

- "And the _____ became flesh, and dwelt among us . . ." (v. 14 NASB).

Jesus Christ Was Fully Human (The Humanity of Christ).

He expressly called Himself and was called "man":

- John 8:40
- Acts 2:22, 23
- Romans 5:15
- 1 Corinthians 15:21
- 1 Timothy 2:5

He expressed human capacities, functions, needs, and emotions. Look up several of these passages, and write down the aspect of Christ's humanity being described:

- Matthew 4:2 _____

- Matthew 8:24 _____

- Matthew 9:36 _____

- Mark 3:5 _____

- Mark 10:21 _____

- Luke 2:52 _____

- John 4:6 _____

- John 11:33, 35 _____

- John 12:27 _____

- John 19:28 _____

He experienced human suffering and death:

- Matthew 26:38
- Luke 22:44
- John 19:30–34
- Hebrews 2:10, 18

Jesus Christ Was Fully God (The Deity of Christ).

He is expressly called God:

- ". . .The only begotten _____ . . ." (John 1:18 NASB).
- ". . . The glorious appearing of our great _____ and _____, Jesus Christ" (Titus 2:13).

He possesses the attributes of God:

- He is **self-existent.** (He does not depend upon anyone or anything for His existence.)

- He is **pre-existent.** (He existed before anything was created.)

- He is **infinitely just.** (He is the only one who has the right to judge or to forgive sin.)

- He is **immutable.** (He does not change.)

- He is the **truth.**

- He is **infinitely loving.**

- He is **holy** (completely set-apart and morally pure).

- He is **omniscient** (all-knowing).

- He is **omnipotent** (all-powerful).

- He is **omnipresent** (present everywhere).

- He is **sovereign.** (He is totally in charge of and in control of everything.)

- He is the **Creator.**

- He is **eternal.** (He has always lived and will always live.)

Look up several of the following references, and select an attribute from the preceding list that is illustrated in each passage. Write that attribute in the space beside the reference.

- Matthew 9:4 _____

- Matthew 28:20 _____

- Mark 2:10, 11 _____

- John 2:24, 25   _____

- John 5:26   _____

- John 6:69   _____

- John 8:58   _____

- John 14:6   _____

- John 17:5   _____

- Ephesians 1:11   _____

- Colossians 1:16   _____

- Colossians 1:17   _____

- Colossians 2:3   _____

- Hebrews 7:26   _____

- Hebrews 13:8   _____

- 1 John 4:8   _____

- Revelation 1:8   _____

- Revelation 3:7   _____

The Three-Fold Ministry of Jesus Christ

- As **Prophet,** beginning at His baptism (Deuteronomy 18:18, 19; Matthew 13:57; 21:11; John 4:19; 6:14; 9:17; Acts 3:22; 7:37)

- As **Priest,** beginning at Calvary (Psalm 110:4; Hebrews 5:6; 6:20; 7:21; 8:1; 9:11)

- As **King** (Psalm 2:6–9; Revelation 19:16)

Christ Is the Atoning Sacrifice for the Sin of Mankind.

His sacrifice is foreshadowed by Old Testament "types" (symbols) that represent Him:

- The coat of skins that cover (Genesis 3:21)

- Abel's lamb (Genesis 4:4)

- The offering of Isaac (Genesis 22:1–18)

- The Passover Lamb (Exodus 12:1–28)

His sacrifice is predicted in Old Testament prophecy:

- The seed of woman (Genesis 3:15)

- The sin offering (Psalm 22)

- The vicarious Savior (Isaiah 53)

- The cut-off Messiah (Daniel 9:26)

- The smitten Shepherd (Zechariah 13:6, 7)

His sacrifice was necessary (Luke 24:26; Galatians 2:21; Hebrews 2:10).

His sacrifice was voluntary (John 10:17–19; Galatians 2:20; Ephesians 5:2; Hebrews 9:14; 10:7–9).

His sacrifice was the **only** sacrifice for sin (Acts 4:12; Romans 3:21–28; Hebrews 1:3; 9:22; 10:10, 12; 1 Peter 3:18).

Christ Was Put to Death on the Cross, but Did Not Stay Dead—He Is the Resurrected One!

- He rose from the dead in fulfillment of prophecy (Psalm 16:10).

- He predicted His own resurrection (Matthew 27:63; Mark 8:31; John 2:19).

- He was raised from the dead by God the Father (Ephesians 1:19, 20; Acts 2:24, 32).

- He arose by His own authority (John 10:18).

- He was made alive by the Holy Spirit (1 Peter 3:18; Romans 8:11).

- He appeared after the Resurrection . . .

    - to Mary (John 20:16).

    - to the men on the Emmaus Road (Luke 24:30, 31).

    - to the disciples in the upper room (John 20:19–23).

    - to Thomas (John 20:24–29).

    - to Peter, John, and five other disciples (John 21:1–12).

    - to more than five hundred people (1 Corinthians 15:6).

Christ Will Return to Judge Humankind, Establish His Kingdom, and Reign for All Eternity.

- ". . . This same Jesus . . . will _____ . . ." (Acts 1:11).

- "For the Lord himself will _____ . . ." (1 Thessalonians 4:16).

- "And when the Chief Shepherd _____, you will receive the crown of glory . . ." (1 Peter 5:4).

- "Look, he is _____ with the clouds, and every eye will see him . . ." (Revelation 1:7).

- Jesus will return to fight the great battle (Revelation 19:11–21).

- "Then I saw a great white _____ and him who was seated on it . . ." (Revelation 20:11).

- Christ will reign for all eternity over the New Heaven and the New Earth (Revelation 21, 22).

- "'Behold, I am _____ soon! . . .'" (Revelation 22:12).

An Experience With God's Son

Expressing Your Praise and Love

The preceding study provides us with right doctrine about Jesus, but we must also let His Holy Spirit lead us into a deeper relationship with Him. Take a few moments to consider in your heart the amazing, incredible, wonderful truth that we have been brought into a relationship with the One of whom all these things are true! How does it make you feel to realize that you have the privilege to know, to love, and to be loved by, such a Savior, such a Friend?

Complete this prayer in your own words:

Lord Jesus, as I think about the incredible privilege of having a relationship with You—the Holy One, the All-Powerful One, the Way, the Truth, and the Life, the One who has loved me so sacrificially—my heart is filled with _____.

(For example: *gratitude, love, joy, praise, a sense of unworthiness, peace, awe, or wonder.*)

Thank You so very much for loving me.

In Your name I pray, Amen.

Ministry Skill

Sharing Your Faith in Christ With Others

"We loved you so much that we were delighted to share with you not only the gospel of God but our lives as well . . ." (1 Thessalonians 2:8).

One of the Follow-up Projects for Chapter 1 was the Ministry Skill of Developing Your Personal Testimony. This project provided a framework for expressing how your relationship with Jesus has made a difference in your life.

As you are being transformed into the image of Jesus, you can count on the Holy Spirit to bring opportunities for you to share your testimony with those who do not yet know Christ as their Savior.

Let the following principles guide not only the sharing of your testimony, but also the relationship-building process that provides the context for people to hear your testimony and to be encouraged to respond to it.

PRINCIPLE #1: JESUS' LIFE AND LOVE IN US PROVIDE THE WITNESS OF A "LIVING LETTER."

"You yourselves are our letter, written on our hearts, known and read by everybody" (2 Corinthians 3:2).

Only as our "walk" matches our "talk" will we have an effective, contagious witness for Christ.

- As we impart His life and love **in spite of people's faults and failures,** we give witness to a Christ who accepts them, who demonstrated His love by dying for us while we were still sinners (Romans 5:8).

- As we impart His life and love **through supportive involvement, caring concern, and practical help,** we give witness to a Christ who bears burdens. "Carry each other's burdens, and in this way you will fulfill the law of Christ" (Galatians 6:2).

- As we impart His life and love **through compassion and comfort** when others are hurting, disappointed, or sorrowful, we give witness to a Christ who ". . . was despised and rejected by men, a man of sorrows, and familiar with suffering . . ." (Isaiah 53:3), who wept for His friend, Mary (John 11:35), and who is often moved with compassion.

PRINCIPLE #2: HIS SPIRIT EMPOWERS OUR WITNESS TO OTHERS CONCERNING THE "GOOD NEWS" OF THE GOSPEL.

"'. . . You will be my witnesses . . .'" (Acts 1:8).

Living out a passionate love for God and gratefully embracing our identity as the "beloved of God" will flow outwardly in our love of others, specifically as we share His good news in the power of the Holy Spirit.

It is good news that . . .

- love comes from God, and God is love (1 John 4:7, 8).

- God is intimately acquainted (caringly involved) with all our ways (Psalm 139:3 NASB).

- our sin keeps us alone—separated from God and others around us (Romans 3:23; 6:23).

- Christ has paid the price for our sin, which keeps us separated from God and from those around us (Romans 3:23, 24; 6:23). His abundant life can be ours both now and for eternity (John 10:10).

- "'Everyone who calls on the name of the Lord will be saved'" (Romans 10:13).

Offer the following prayer in closing:

Jesus, I need You. I receive Your forgiveness and Your love. I receive Your care and acceptance of me. I give to You my life, my future, my all. Thank You for loving me, forgiving me, and changing me. I yield to Your Spirit within me. Change me so that I may express You to others around me.

In your Name, Amen.

Scripture Memory

2 Corinthians 3:18 NASB

"But we all, with unveiled face, beholding as in a mirror the glory of the Lord, are being transformed into the same image from glory to glory, just as from the Lord, the Spirit."

Chapter 6

Transformed by Experiencing Fellowship

A t different times, Jesus declared to the disciples both, "'I am the light of the world . . .'" (John 8:12) and, "'You are the light of the world . . .'" (Matthew 5:14). Undoubtedly the disciples found this paradox confusing. Maybe at some point, in an attempt to clear up the matter, they asked Him, "Master, are **You** the light of the world, or are **we** the light of the world?" Perhaps Jesus responded, "Yes!"

In this chapter, we will explore the truth that we, the saints, have the privilege and calling to reveal God's light. This is a key way in which we express the glory that dwells within us.

> **As we encounter God in and through other believers, we are transformed.**

Encountering God's light in one another is a significant aspect of the process of spiritual formation. As we encounter God in and through other believers, we are transformed. This is why genuine fellowship is not optional; it is a necessary requirement for the spiritual transformation of every believer!

THE MYSTERY OF REAL FELLOWSHIP

To unravel the mystery of genuine fellowship (*koinonia*), we will begin with a familiar passage: "And my God will meet all your needs according to his glorious riches in Christ Jesus" (Philippians 4:19).

First, it is noteworthy that Paul's expression, "my God" is rare in the New Testament. It is almost as if Paul, by using the phrase "my God," is bragging on God. He seems to be excited to declare that his God is a God who meets needs. Perhaps he is saying . . .

- if you have a "sin-inspecting god" who is always trying to catch you doing something wrong, I am sad for you because my God—the real God—is seeking to meet your needs!

- if you have a "disappointed god" who is constantly communicating that he is disappointed with you, I am sad for you because my God is longing to meet your needs!

- if you have a "distant god" who does not even seem to notice you, I am sad for you because my God notices and cares for even the birds and the flowers—and much more so for you!

> **The same Jesus who longs to meet us in worship, prayer, meditation, and solitude also wants to bless, encourage, and change us as we encounter Him in others.**

Walking in the light of the real God, the God whom Paul "brags on," was the subject of Chapter 5. We saw that, as the Holy Spirit leads us into fresh encounters with Christ, the deepening of our intimacy with Him transforms, sustains, and empowers us. But there is more! The same Jesus who longs to meet us in worship, prayer, meditation, and solitude also wants to bless, encourage, and change us as we encounter Him **in others.**

For many years, I thought I knew, understood, and "believed" Philippians 4:19, only to be confronted one day with the truth of 1 Corinthians 8:2 (NASB): "If anyone supposes that he knows anything, he has not yet known as he ought to know." My typical image of Philippians 4:19 was that God had His "glorious riches" hidden away in heaven in a big cabinet, closet, or safe, and when you were in need, the Holy Spirit mysteriously "unlocked" the source, took some of the riches of His glory, and somehow "zapped" you with it. If you were hurting and in need of comfort, you prayed, and He zapped you with comfort. If you were discouraged, you sought after Him in faith, and He zapped you with encouragement.

There is no doubt that the Holy Spirit does directly bless us at times with comfort, encouragement, and the like. But during a time of meditation on Ephesians 1:18, the Holy Spirit radically changed my image of His glorious riches and ushered me into a deeper understanding of true fellowship among His saints. As I read the words, "I pray also that the eyes of your heart may be enlightened . . ." the Spirit seemed to whisper, "This prayer is for you." I then read the remainder of the verse: "in order that you may know . . . the riches of His glorious inheritance in the saints."

My eyes fixed on the words "in the saints." Then the Spirit opened the "eyes of my heart." I was struck by the truth that many of God's glorious riches are already in His saints! The Lord seemed to say, "David, some of the acceptance you need in the midst of your self-doubt, I am longing to give you through my people. Some of the encouragement, care, and affirmation you need when you grow weary in well-doing, I want to provide you through My body. It is still My acceptance, My encouragement, My care, but I want to share it with you by expressing My glory through My church. I will still be providing for you, but I will work in and through others to do so."

So how does Christ actually transform us as we experience His light and riches through the saints? How does He make us more like Himself through our relationships with each other?

THE TRANSFORMING POWER OF FELLOWSHIP

"Let us not give up meeting together . . . " (Hebrews 10:25).

Receiving the Light of God Through Others Transforms Us.

"'. . . Freely you have received . . .'" (Matthew 10:8).

This scripture urges us to be mindful of what we have received from God. As you reflect on God's gifts, you will soon realize that you have often received from Him through His people. This receiving of the light of God through others is part of the process by which God makes us more like Jesus.

As I mentioned previously, my heart was softened by God's acceptance (which was manifested in the loving care of my Spirit-filled grandfather) when I was rebellious, fast-driving, 15-year-old. But I did not seriously consider the claims of Christ until I was 21.

My wife, Teresa, started attending a local church out of loneliness. She then suggested that I might need to go! I agreed, on two conditions: we sit at the rear of the church, and we leave before the preacher "caught us" at the back door. Those were my rules.

> I began to realize that the Christian life was not so much about "believing right" and "behaving right." Rather, I found that it was about having an intimate, loving relationship with a Person—Jesus.

Sitting in that church, with my long hair, sandaled feet, and rebellious attitude, I would look around and think, *There's bound to be somebody else here who doesn't like these people any more than I do!* So I started looking for a fellow rebel.

I met the church custodian, a fellow named Paul, and I thought, *Surely he feels picked on and put upon by these people!* Amazingly, he reached out to me, and we started hanging out together.

> **Receiving riches such as His acceptance through others is used by the Holy Spirit to transform us more and more into the likeness of the One who is infinitely accepting: "Accept one another, then, just as Christ accepted you . . ." (Romans 15:7).**

But Paul was not the rebel for which I was looking. Instead, he proved to be a kind-hearted man who allowed me to see the reality of his relationship with Jesus Christ. I was finishing my first degree in nuclear physics, and he was a custodian with little formal education, yet he would take his Bible and teach me by simply sharing his heart. Through these conversations with Paul, I began to realize that the Christian life was not so much about "believing right" and "behaving right." Rather, I found that it was about having an intimate, loving relationship with a Person—Jesus.

Paul got to know me. He entered into a relationship with me by asking questions about my classes and interests. He also allowed me to know him. He was vulnerable with his life and his heart. He shared with me that though he was an ordained pastor, he was serving in that church as a custodian because he had some pain and challenges in his own life. Yet he continued to serve the Lord even though he could not serve as a pastor at that time.

I had never had a Christian be that vulnerable with personal pain. The Christians I had been around only wanted to talk about their correct doctrine and their right behavior. Few would share their struggles and failures, their challenges and imperfections. But Paul was both Christian and "real." Through his life and our friendship, God began to reveal to me that a relationship with Jesus could be real and work even in the midst of pain and struggles.

Paul genuinely cared for me as well. One day, after I had helped him paint swings on the church playground, he said, "Hey, before you go, would it be all right if I prayed for your quantum mechanics test?" He put his hands on me and prayed that God would help me with the exam. Paul might not even have known what quantum mechanics was, but he was praying to the God who did!

The light of God was shining into my life through Paul, one of God's saints. I received some of the "glorious riches" of God's acceptance and encouragement through Paul, and not long thereafter, I received Christ as my Savior. As I continued to experience God's acceptance of me through Paul and others, the Holy Spirit began to transform me more and more into the likeness of Christ. I began to desire to accept others as Jesus had accepted me (Romans 15:7).

Have there been people who have entered your life, loved you, and cared for you in ways that touched you, challenged you, and even changed you? That is the power of fellowship! We receive God's glorious riches through His people, in order that we might be made more like our Savior.

An Experience With God's People

"Each one should use whatever gift he has received to serve others, faithfully administering God's grace in its various forms" (1 Peter 4:10).

God's glorious riches are simply dimensions or facets of His grace that we "administer" as we serve others. These riches include His acceptance, His encouragement, His comfort, His respect, His approval, His support, and many other things that we all need—things that we often receive through others, but that are ultimately from God.

Consider the saints who have blessed and challenged you through sharing the glorious riches of Jesus with you. Then complete the following sentences:

"I have received . . .

> God's **acceptance** through _____,
> *particularly when he/she/they* _____.

> God's **encouragement** through _____,
> *particularly when he/she/they* _____.

> God's **comfort** through _____,
> *particularly when he/she/they* _____.

(For example: *I have received God's encouragement through my friend Mike, particularly when he told me that he has seen how God has gifted me to counsel others in order to help them experience God's truth.*)

"And let us consider how we may spur one another on toward love and good deeds" (Hebrews 10:24).

Pause to reflect on how you have received God's glorious riches through others, and how you have been challenged to become a person who shares His riches in turn. Complete as many of these sentences as describe you:

The **acceptance** *I have received from* _____ *has challenged me to become more accepting in these ways:* _____
_____
_____.

The **encouragement** *I have received from* _____ *has challenged me to become more encouraging in these ways:* _____
_____
_____.

The **comfort** *I have received from* _____ *has challenged me to become more comforting in these ways:* _____
_____
_____.

The _____ *I have received from* _____ *has challenged me to become more* _____ *in these ways:* _____
_____.

(For example: *The **acceptance** I have received from my small group leader has challenged me to become more accepting in these ways: Even though my younger brother is very different from me, I now take initiative to spend time with him, trying to understand his point of view by asking questions and listening carefully, and also just having some fun together.*)

Share your responses with your partner or small group, rejoicing together over the ways in which loving fellowship encourages our transformation into the image of Jesus.

Giving the Light of God to Others Transforms Us.

"'. . . freely give'" (Matthew 10:8).

True fellowship requires that we not only receive of God's glorious riches, but that we share His multi-faceted grace with others. We participate in the Spirit's work of making us more like Jesus not just by "freely receiving," but also by "freely giving." This might involve . . .

- accepting those who are very different from us, sometimes in spite of their faults and failures (Romans 15:7).

- comforting others by just hurting with them, refraining from giving advice, pep talks, or pat assurances that God will "work things out for good." Just as Jesus wept with His friend Mary in the midst of her pain, we can demonstrate tenderness and compassion simply with our presence, a few empathetic words, or tears (2 Corinthians 1:3, 4; John 11:35).

- giving attention and care to those who inconvenience us, interrupt us, or in some way present themselves as distractions in our path (1 Corinthians 12:25, 26).

As we are challenged to give in these ways, we bump right into the limitations and ugliness of our own self-focus—what Scripture calls "the flesh." We then realize that the Spirit's sanctifying, transforming work is our only hope of becoming like Jesus. We will not accomplish this through self-effort; it will not be possible by our own might or power, but only by His Spirit (Zechariah 4:6).

As we are challenged to give in these ways, we bump right into the limitations and ugliness of our own self-focus—what Scripture calls "the flesh." We then realize that the Spirit's sanctifying, transforming work is our only hope of becoming like Jesus.

Recently, the Spirit confronted me with the impatience and coldness that I had often demonstrated toward my wife, Teresa—specifically when she would interrupt me in the midst of my more "eternally focused" initiatives. I would be excitedly preparing for some ministry event—a conference Teresa and I were to lead, a significant meeting with denominational leaders, or a team meeting with our staff—and she would disrupt my concentration, focus, and preparation with what seemed to me like the most trivial concerns. It might be a family financial matter, a comment about the need for us to plan a long-delayed social time with another couple, or the dreaded question, "What should we do about dinner tonight?" I am ashamed to admit that I tended to respond to such "interruptions" with impatience and insensitivity, often accompanied by the rationalization that I was simply attempting to give priority to "kingdom matters" rather than more mundane concerns.

For too many years, I failed to realize that these encounters with Teresa were the Spirit's invitation and challenge for me to freely give some of God's glorious riches to my wife:

- I was invited to give His support in order to help bear the burden of Teresa's financial concerns (Galatians 6:2). Too often, my insensitive responses left her alone in her concern. Christ bore His cross to Calvary for me, but in my fleshly self-focus, I struggled just to share a moment of supportive dialogue with my wife. The Spirit's transforming work was clearly needed in me.

- I was granted the opportunity to give His care, thus joining Teresa in her care for others. She was taking thought of our friends and desiring to give priority to being there for them. Meanwhile, I was supposedly focusing on "eternal things," yet was largely ignoring my responsibility to care for our friends. Jesus was caring, Teresa was caring, and I was inconvenienced and impatient. My need to grow into His image was becoming more apparent.

> **Through common challenges to truly give to others, His Spirit will reveal much-needed works of making us like Jesus.**

- I was challenged to give His security in order to ease the strain of Teresa's insecurities. To me, "What should we do about dinner tonight?" meant "Do you want fish or fast food?" What an irrelevant question in the face of my "kingdom focus"! But to Teresa it meant, "I am desiring the security that comes from planning my day around giving priority to you, David." She was thinking of me, and I was thinking only of myself. My need for brokenness and transformation was obvious.

How about you? Have you had recent or recurring opportunities to give His support, His care, or His security to those around you? How did you respond? Do not miss the important truth that such opportunities are invitations and challenges to become more like Jesus, to be transformed into His image as we walk in the light of true fellowship.

An Experience With God's Word

"Then one of the synagogue rulers, named Jairus, came there. Seeing Jesus, he fell at his feet and pleaded earnestly with him, 'My little daughter is dying. Please come and put your hands on her so that she will be healed and live.' So Jesus went with him . . ." (Mark 5:22–24).

Notice the significance of Christ and the disciples heading off to minister at the home of a synagogue ruler. Imagine the disciples' excitement: "Finally, a breakthrough with the synagogue officials has come! This is the opportunity we have been waiting for—Jesus will perform a miracle of healing for Jairus' daughter, and surely many doors of ministry will open!"

Mark's account continues: ". . . A large crowd followed and pressed around him. And a woman was there who had been subject to bleeding for twelve years. She had suffered a great deal under the care of many doctors and had spent all she had, yet instead of getting better she grew worse. When she heard about Jesus, she came up behind him in the crowd and touched his cloak. . . . Immediately her bleeding stopped. . . . At once Jesus realized that power had gone out from him. He turned around in the crowd and asked, 'Who touched my clothes?'

'You see the people crowding against you,' his disciples answered, 'and yet you can ask, "Who touched me?"'

But Jesus kept looking around to see who had done it" (vv. 24–32).

Notice the contrast between Jesus and the disciples. Jesus stops, sensitive to what has happened and wanting to connect with the woman who touched Him. The disciples, in contrast, seem irritated. "What do you mean, who touched You?" they ask. You can sense in these words their impatience and frustration. Their agenda has been interrupted. Undoubtedly, they were thinking, *We need to get to Jairus' house! We may miss this opportunity!*

God used this passage to give me additional light regarding my reactions to Teresa's untimely comments. He impressed me with this thought: "David, you are so busy, so focused on what

you think is ministry, that you miss opportunities to minister. I have stopped to notice Teresa's needs, but you are irritated that we have stopped!"

The Spirit was showing me the real me.

How about you?

Pause now to reflect on your own life, career, calling, ministry, or pursuits. Perhaps you are occasionally interrupted just as you are excitedly heading off to do "important" things. People near you need you!

Who might some of these "interrupting" people be in your life? Maybe your family members? Close friends? Co-workers? Small group members? About what might they typically "interrupt" you?

I am sometimes interrupted by . . .

_____ *concerning* _____.
_____ *concerning* _____.
_____ *concerning* _____.

Do you, at times, feel inconvenienced or even irritated because these people need you? Consider what these people might really need. Could they be needing . . .

- God's support, shared through you?

- God's care, shared through you?

- God's security, shared through you?

What they really need are God's glorious riches, given through you. You have freely received these riches, and you are now being challenged to freely give them. God's support, care, security, encouragement, patience, kindness, and acceptance are in you. These riches are not really just for you. God's desire is that you would share them, thus extending His presence and expressing His glory.

Take a moment to be still before the Lord. Listen to His Spirit as you reflect on your encounters with those around you.

Recall some of God's "glorious riches":

- acceptance

- attention

- encouragement

- comfort

- care

- support

- patience

- kindness

- _____ (You add one!)

Complete this sentence:

When _____ is needing _____, I may sometimes feel inconvenienced, interrupted, and/or irritated.

(For example: *When my son is needing attention, I may sometimes feel irritated.*)

"Confess your faults one to another, and pray one for another, that ye may be healed" (James 5:16 KJV).

Now share your response with your partner or small group. Ask your partner or group members to pray that God's Spirit might change you, freeing you from irritation and frustration at life's interruptions, and making you more accepting, encouraging, comforting, and supportive. Take turns praying one for another, that you might be healed, transformed, and perfected into the image of Christ.

Your prayer might sound something like the following:

Dear Lord, I pray for _____. *I ask that You would help him to be more*

_____

_____ *with* _____. *May the*
Holy Spirit empower Christ's love through this saint. By Your Spirit, bring freedom so that
he might give in this way.

In Jesus' name, Amen.

The Rest of the Story

Let us return to Mark's account of Jesus' actions on His way to the home of Jairus:

"Then the woman, knowing what had happened to her, came and fell at his feet and, trembling with fear, told him the whole truth. He said to her, 'Daughter, your faith has healed you. Go in peace and be freed from your suffering.'

While Jesus was still speaking, some men came from the house of Jairus, the synagogue ruler. 'Your daughter is dead,' they said. 'Why bother the teacher any more?'

Ignoring what they said, Jesus told the synagogue ruler, 'Don't be afraid; just believe. . . .'

'Little girl, I say to you, get up!'" (Mark 5:33–36, 41).

With these words, even greater blessing and ministry than the disciples could have anticipated takes place at Jairus' house—his daughter, who had died, returns to life!

Like the disciples, we need to learn that stopping to give to those who interrupt us does not mean that we lose out on God's best in our ministry, calling, or other

> **Like the disciples, we need to learn that stopping to give to those who interrupt us does not mean that we lose out on God's best in our ministry, calling, or other pursuits.**

pursuits. Rather, such seeming "interruptions" become occasions of fellowship through which we are transformed by the Spirit into the likeness of Christ as we walk in the light of His people!

What This Fellowship Looks Like

When we come together as parts of the body that are all attached to Jesus Christ, the Head, we must not focus on comparing how much you know to how much I know. We are not to come together thinking, *I wonder if I can impress somebody tonight?* We must gather with the realization that we are bringing God's glorious riches into our place of meeting.

Think about some of the contexts in which you gather with other parts of the body. Might there be someone in your church who could benefit from you being a good steward of God's riches? Is there someone in your small group, care group, Women's Mentoring Group, or Men's Coaching Ministry who could benefit from the acceptance you have received, the support that the Spirit of God has given you, or the encouragement that God has blessed you with?

As you fellowship with God and dwell in His Word, the Spirit may take a particular thought or passage of Scripture and encourage your heart, motivating you to walk in His light. As you come to understand true fellowship, you will realize that such encouragement is not only for you, but is meant to be shared with other members of the body. So as you arrive at your next breakfast appointment with the friend you are mentoring, or the next meeting of your small group, you are ready to encourage others with the encouragement that you have already received: "I was just encouraged by the Lord yesterday, and I can't help but wonder if maybe there is a ministry of encouragement that the Spirit would want to bring into your life." We are now moving out of the darkness of irrelevant religion into the wonder of genuine fellowship (*koinonia*).

"TRANSFORMATION BLESSINGS" OF TRUE FELLOWSHIP

As we are transformed into the image of Jesus through sharing His glorious riches with each other, we can anticipate certain specific blessings as a result of our fellowship.

The Blessing of Seeing Christ as He Really Is

In Chapter 2, we noted that we are all hindered, at times, from seeing Christ clearly. All of us have misconceptions about who He really is. One blessing that we receive as we walk in the light of fellowship is the opportunity to see Christ more clearly by encountering Him in the lives of other saints:

"No one has ever seen God. But if we love each other, God lives in us, and His love has been brought to full expression through us" (1 John 4:12 NLT).

True fellowship, in which we genuinely love each other, enables the "full expression" of God's love in and through us. As we experience God's love through the love of others, we see Him as He really is. As we receive acceptance from others, we see the God of gracious acceptance. Through the comfort of another human being, we see evidence of the One who is ". . . the Father of compassion and the God of all comfort" (2 Corinthians 1:3).

> **True fellowship, in which we genuinely love each other, enables the "full expression" of God's love in and through us. As we experience God's love through the love of others, we see Him as He really is.**

Just as we receive this blessing of seeing God **through** others, so we are called to express His presence **to** others, giving testimony to His glorious riches in order that they might see Him more clearly in turn.

A Testimony of Seeing Christ as He Really Is

In our ministry leaders' conferences, Teresa and I often share an example of the transforming power of seeing God as He really is. Teresa normally shares something like this, concerning one of our trips overseas:

"We were on our way to the airport to return home from England. It was a good day—David and I hadn't had a fight (I don't know about you all, but we still occasionally have fights), I wasn't anxious, and we weren't running late. In fact, David had worked hard to make sure we would be early to the airport. Everything seemed to be going well.

"There was one slight problem, however: I was thirsty. I thought to myself, *There's a petrol station not far ahead. It is on the opposite side of the road, but traffic is not too bad this morning, and David and I are a little ahead of schedule. So I think we can stop to get a Coke.*

"But this is how my words came out: 'David, there's a petrol station not too far up the road if you would like to stop and get you a Coke.'"

My part of the sharing typically includes the rest of the story:

"Now that is the kind of sentence that I had been hearing for more than 35 years of marriage—Would **I** like to stop and get **me** a Coke?

"Well, we had had a good few days together, and we hadn't had an argument that morning, so I thought, *I'm going to take this one on.* So I just looked at her and I said, 'No, I'm fine.' Now at that point, I obviously had her attention. However, I know her well enough to know that I should not leave her like that very long. So after about five seconds I took her by the hand, looked at her, and said, 'But I'd love to stop and get you one because you're worth stopping for.'"

Over the course of our marriage, Teresa, out of her anxiety, would often say things like, "Would you like to stop and get you a Coke?" But for three and a half decades, what she would typically sense from me in response was frustration and irritation. We might stop and get the Coke, but my body language and demeanor would communicate to her the exasperated question, "Why don't you just say what you mean?"

> **Beside the road that day, the Spirit tugged at my heart to say, "David, I'm feeling compassion for Teresa. Would you like to join Me?"**

But this day was different. We pulled over to the side of the road, and she began to cry. I began to cry. We just cried together. As we sat there, the Holy Spirit challenged me to better express Christ's heart to my wife. I am certain that for many years God had heard Teresa speak those sentences, and that He had been moved with compassion for her because she was anxious and uncertain about how to ask for a soft drink. At times, she even questioned, "Am I worth stopping for?" For all of those years, Christ was compassionate toward her, but I was frustrated with her.

The Spirit tugged at my heart and said, "David, I am feeling compassion for Teresa. Would you like to join Me?" I then realized that, for years, my obvious irritation had communicated to my wife a false image of who God is. Beside the road that day, God's Spirit did a much-needed work of encouraging Christ-likeness in me in order that I might better express to Teresa who the real God is: "O Honey, the real God is not mad at you. The real God is not irritated at you. The real God is compassionate toward you."

None of us have seen God, but His love can be brought to full expression through us. What if one of the reasons we are on this planet is to so live and love that a few other people around us see Christ for who He really is? Would that give eternal meaning to your life? This is one of the significant blessings of fellowship.

> **What if one of the reasons we are on this planet is to so live and love that a few other people around us see Christ for who He really is? Would that give eternal meaning to your life?**

The Blessing of Experiencing Our True Identity

The second blessing of fellowship is that, upon seeing more clearly who God is, we can discover who we really are.

Our world shares with us a lie that who you are is determined by your performance, thereby keeping many in the bondage of what one of our denominational leaders calls "who-do-ism"— the belief that who I am is equal to what I do.

In our society, when I meet someone, I say, "Hi, my name is David Ferguson. What's yours?" And what is the next question I ask? Isn't it, "What do you do?" Then, having heard what the person does, my self-focused flesh begins to assess the question, "How does what I do compare to what you do?"

The testimony of the gospel is that your true identity is not determined by what you do. But how are we going to loose the shackles of performance-based worth? How can we refute the world's lie that our life's value is tied to what we acquire, accomplish, and achieve?

One of the things the Spirit of God is longing to do through genuine fellowship among believers is to break the bondage of "who-do-ism." Our loving relationships with one another affirm our identity as God's beloved. He then sends us forth as ambassadors of this good news to those who do not know Christ. God's declaration of our identity and unconditional worth is communicated as we bless people with His care and love, even though they have not done anything to deserve or merit it.

God declared our infinite, unconditional worth at Calvary: "But God demonstrates his own love for us in this: While we were still sinners, Christ died for us" (Romans 5:8). His Spirit desires to empower our expression of this same love one to another. That's one of the blessings of fellowship.

There are going to be times when fellow-believers fail, when we hurt each other, when we sin against each other. At such times, the body of Christ must step forward and say, "We see the wrongness and inappropriateness of your behavior, but we are here to love you as God loves you and us. We will love you no matter what, so how can we work together to address this problem?" As we extend grace in this way, we free people from the prison of performance-based worth, thus enabling them to sense, "This is who I am—I am the beloved of God."

> **One of the things the Spirit of God is longing to do through genuine fellowship among believers is to break the bondage of "who-do-ism." Our loving relationships with one another affirm our identity as God's beloved.**

An Example of Love Affirming True Identity

I have a friend who is the pastor of a large and growing church. If you were to ask him, "How have you seen God grow this phenomenal church?" he might tell you about his Friday morning phone calls. Every Friday morning, he drives to the church and asks the Lord, "Lord, on my 20-minute commute, would You remind me of a few people in this church for whom I am especially grateful?" When he gets to the church, he spends the next two hours just calling those saints and saying something like, "On my drive in this morning, I was reminded by the Lord how blessed we are to have you as a part of our fellowship, and I just wanted to call and tell you that. Have a blessed day! Goodbye."

Do you think those people are shocked by that kind of phone call? I promise you that they are because, like many believers, they probably think, *If anybody calls me from the church, it is only because they are going to ask me to do something or give some money.* Sadly, what many Christians cynically expect to hear is, "I'm so glad God sent you to our church . . . by the way, we need help in the nursery," or "We're looking for someone to sing in the choir." But by offering sincere expressions of love and appreciation without making high-pressure requests for assistance, this pastor has captured the possibilities of Christ's startling love, and is working to restore to the saints their identity as God's beloved.

The Blessing of Loving Those Nearest Us

". . . Let us run with endurance the race that is set before us" (Hebrews 12:1 NASB).

Scripture speaks of us running not a solo sprint, but a team relay, with each of us, at times, being encouraged toward "love and good deeds" by one another (10:24).

Years ago, during the U.S. Special Olympics, TV viewers were brought to tears during the 100-yard dash. When the starter's gun sounded, the runners, most of whom had Downs Syndrome, took off down the track. About midway through the race, one young boy stumbled and fell, sprawling on the track.

As the crowds present and the millions who were viewing the scene on TV looked on in sympathy, they were given an unforgettable lesson in the power of fellowship by the other runners: One by one, they stopped running and went back to the fallen boy. Helping him to his feet, the crowd of runners headed off again toward the finish line, crossing it together arm-in-arm.

> **As we are transformed by the One who is love (1 John 4:8) into His image, love must be expressed in our homes, marriages, families, and friendships.**

This sort of mutual encouragement is desperately needed among us, especially as we are challenged to express God's presence and love to our nearest "neighbors." As we are transformed by the One who **is** love (1 John 4:8) into His image, love must be expressed in our homes, marriages, families, and friendships.

Over the years, during times of mutual sharing or small group prayer, fellow believers, who knew and loved me, have asked me questions such as, "When is the next fun time you and Teresa have planned?" or "How is your Thursday night family time coming along?" These friends knew that I often struggled to give priority to those near me. My invitation for God to bring people into my life to encourage my accountability in this area created a safe and supportive framework of fellowship within which they could ask these kinds of questions and I could receive them and respond vulnerably to them. We all need such loving inquiry at times. God longs for us to turn back for each struggling runner so that we all can finish well together.

Pause and Reflect

Who has been given permission by you to inquire about the important matters of your life?

Who have you invited to help stimulate you toward love and good deeds, especially with those nearest to you?

Has your heart been yielded to receive such inquiry and encouragement with gratitude, or are you defensive and resistant?

The Blessing of Partnering Together in the Great Commission

The word "fellowship" (*koinonia*) refers to caring connectedness within the body of Christ. But it also connotes partnering together for a larger purpose. Our fellowship is intended to transform us in order that we might join together to pursue the eternal purposes of the kingdom, including the undertaking of Christ's Great Commission to make disciples of all nations (Matthew 28:19, 20).

When Jesus said, "'. . . Follow me . . . and I will make you fishers of men'" (4:19), what image would have come to the disciples' minds? They would not have pictured an individual trying to catch fish on his own, but rather a crew or team casting nets into the sea together. Imagine trying to carry a large, wet net filled with several hundred pounds of fish. Your resolve to be self-reliant

> When Jesus said, "Follow me . . . and I will make you fishers of men" (Matthew 4:19), what image would have come to the disciples' minds? They would not have pictured an individual trying to catch fish on his own, but rather a crew or team casting nets into the sea together.

would be broken very quickly! Our only hope of having a major impact for the cause of Christ in the unbelieving world is to function together in *koinonia*, realizing that some of God's glorious riches are in each of us. Together, we can cast the net of fellowship in order to see eternal things done for the kingdom.

The Blessing of Being Loved Through Reproof and Correction

Because we love one another, and because our hearts and lives have been tenderly knit together in fellowship, we are free to lovingly share truth that challenges, confronts, and reproves. At times, some of the glorious riches we must share will be caring yet honest words of correction like Christ shared with the woman caught in adultery: "'. . . Neither do I condemn you . . . Go now and leave your life of sin'" (John 8:11). Because I love you, I must share God's loving concern for you.

Prior to becoming a Christian, I was good at being a "lost" person. So when I gave God control of my life, I felt like I had to make up for lost time. My zeal and passion were quite noticeable in the context of my somewhat passive church, which was just beginning to embrace the energy of the "Jesus movement" of the late 1960s. As a result, I was entrusted much too early with roles and responsibilities beyond my maturity. At 23, I was ordained as a deacon in this church. I was off trying to share the gospel with others, yet I still had much to learn.

I remember sharing with Paul, my church custodian friend, one day: "Paul, as I have pursued ministry and spent time on the university campus, I have become convinced that I have to do a better job of sharing Christ with other people."

What I really wanted Paul to say was, "Don't be too hard on yourself. Given how young you are in the faith, you're doing great!" Instead, he said, "I'll pray for you." When he said that, I thought, *What do you mean, pray for me? All I'm looking for is a little affirmation!*

When Paul said, "I'll pray for you," he meant it. I never recall him saying those words without immediately laying his hands on me and starting to pray! This occasion was no different. We were standing in the church foyer, people were passing us on their way out, and the church custodian grabbed me by the shoulder with one hand, raised the other hand, and loudly prayed that I might start sharing my faith more boldly.

His public prayer was just what I needed to gently reprove and correct my pride, but I did not quite see it that way. What was happening in my heart was not pretty. There I was, simply trying to be vulnerable about my ministry struggles (while really just wanting kudos), and Paul had the audacity not only to say, "Let's pray about that," but to begin praying right there in front of everybody!

I left as quickly as I could, got in my car, and went home thinking, *I have just been embarrassed. Here I am—a deacon serving these people—and I have the custodian praying over me, trying to make me an evangelist!*

> **His public prayer was just what I needed to gently reprove and correct my pride, but I did not quite see it that way.**

My anger lasted throughout the rest of that Sunday, and carried over into Monday. When I got out of class on Monday afternoon, I thought, *I'm going to the church. I'm going to find Paul. I'm going to talk to him about what he did. I'm upset.*

I drove into the church parking lot and saw a Scotty's Plumbing van. Paul had gotten involved in Scotty's life, helping his family find a place to live and assisting them with the expenses of groceries and shoes for the kids. Paul had been loving Scotty like he had been loving me.

I walked into the church and began stalking through the halls, looking for Paul. *We're going to have it out right here,* I thought. *I'm just not appreciative of his insensitivity.* But I could not find Paul anywhere. As I walked toward the front of the worship center, I heard voices—Paul and Scotty were underneath the baptistry. Apparently, there was a leak, and Scotty was there to fix it.

That didn't stop me. I was going to find Paul, and we were going to talk. I got on my knees and began to crawl underneath the baptistry. Then I realized that the two men were praying. Paul was leading Scotty to Christ underneath the baptistry.

What do you think the Holy Spirit did in the heart of this young deacon? Can you imagine what took place next? Prostrate on the floor, I cried out to God, who had just taken some of the glorious riches in one of His saints and confronted my sin. He had challenged my pride and immaturity through Paul's example.

That's the potential of fellowship empowered by the Holy Spirit. Oh, that we might walk in the light of fellowship in order to be transformed into His likeness with ever-increasing glory (2 Corinthians 3:18).

An Experience With God's Son

"'. . . Everyone who is fully trained will be like his teacher'" (Luke 6:40).

Imagine Christ standing before you—the only true Teacher (Matthew 23:10), the One who is love (1 John 4:8), the God of all comfort (2 Corinthians 1:3, 4), the One who is humble and gentle (Matthew 11:29, 30). Imagine that He invites you to become like Him, to express His life and love, to extend the light of His presence in a dark world.

Though you may not yet fully know all the transforming work that will be needed in your life, consider yielding in your heart to Christ's invitation. Offer the following prayer with your partner or small group as an expression of the longing of your hearts and your mutual commitment to walk in the light of fellowship:

Lord Jesus, as You see those things in my character, behavior, or attitudes that are distracting to my expression of You to those around me, please bring others into my life to lovingly point them out. Prepare my heart by Your Spirit to receive Your counsel, Your reproof, and Your correction from those whom You send. I want to be changed. I want to be more like You.

In Your name, Amen.

Extending the presence of God into every situation and conversation becomes the passion of the true disciple. This passion births a longing to hear from God through His Word, His Son, and His saints, so that we might then yield to Him.

But what results might the disciple anticipate from this "exercise program" of walking in God's light? What will our spiritual "muscle tone" look like? In Chapter 7, we will explore three significant aspects of strengthening the "inner man" in order that we might clearly reflect God's glory.

CHAPTER 6 FOLLOW-UP PROJECTS
1. **Bible Doctrine:** The Light of God's People, the Church
2. **Life Application:** Others-Centered Love
3. **Scripture Memory:** 1 John 4:12

Bible Doctrine

The Light of God's People, the Church

CHRIST'S CHURCH AND THE POSSIBILITIES OF FELLOWSHIP

Instructions: To help cement key concepts in your mind, certain blanks have been left for you to complete. As you read through this doctrinal study, fill in those blanks with the word or words that you think are most appropriate.

In the New Testament, the word *church* is a translation of the Greek word *ekklesia*. It refers in a general sense to any gathering or assembly of people. It was used in a secular sense for a group of people assembling together for public discussion or business.

The word is actually a combination of the words *ek* (which means "out") and *kaleo* (which means to "call" or "summon"). Literally then, *ekklesia* refers to the "called-out ones."

The first appearance of this word in the New Testament has great significance for our understanding of God's transforming love. The Gospel of Matthew records a discussion between Jesus and His disciples concerning who Jesus is. After the disciples relate some popular opinions about His identity, Jesus pointedly asks them, "'But who do **you** say I am?'" Peter responds, "'You are the Christ, the Son of the living God.'" Jesus then replies to Peter, "'Blessed are you, Simon son of Jonah, for this was not revealed to you by man, but by my Father in heaven'" (See Matthew 16:13–20.)

How did Peter come to know that Christ was the Son of the living God? It was because the Father _____ this critically important truth to him.

In the same way, we enter into Christ's church by first having Christ revealed to us: "'All things have been committed to me by my Father. No one knows who the Son is except the Father, and no one knows who the Father is except the Son and those to whom the Son chooses to _____ him'" (Luke 10:22).

Then we must yield to Him, just as Peter did through his declaration, "'You are the Christ'": "'Everyone who calls on the name of the Lord will be saved'" (Romans 10:13).

In response to the Father's revealing and Peter's yielding, Christ declares, "'. . . On this rock I will build _____ _____'" (Matthew 16:18).

Here, in the context of this revealing, yielding dynamic, we find the first use of *ekklesia* in the New Testament. Notice that Christ refers to these "called-out ones" as _____ church. There may be other gatherings and assemblies of people, but Jesus is identifying the church as **His** called-out ones.

The following key principles are relevant to our understanding of how to live as a fellowship of believers, as Christ's church:

1. As Christ's church, we have been *called out* from the world and *called to* live for Him.

   • "'They are not of the_____, even as I am not of it'" (John 17:16).

   • Our fellowship together is to provide an environment of mutual encouragement and exhortation, that we might ". . . live a life worthy of the _____ . . ." we have received (Ephesians 4:1).

2. As the "body of Christ," the church relates to Christ as the Head (Ephesians 4:15; Colossians 2:19).

   • "And he is the _____ of the body, the _____ . . ." (Colossians 1:18).

   • True fellowship flows from common submission (yielding) to Christ as our Head, with each member of the body exercising specific gifts and ministries as He sovereignly wills (1 Corinthians 12:4–7).

   • True fellowship leads to a recognition that, though it is organized, the church as Christ's body is a living, relational organism, not merely an organization.

3. As the "temple of God," the church is God's building, with Christ as the cornerstone (1 Corinthians 3:9–17; 1 Timothy 3:15; 1 Peter 2:4–8).

   - "Consequently, you are no longer foreigners and aliens, but fellow citizens with God's people and members of God's household . . . with Christ Jesus himself as the chief _____. In him the whole building is joined together and rises to become a holy _____ in the Lord" (Ephesians 2:19–21).

   - This "temple" is a visible expression in this world of God's unseen kingdom.

   - Our fellowship together is to give evidence of God's glory and purity, realizing that we have become the temple for the indwelling of the Holy Spirit (1 Corinthians 6:19).

4. As the "bride of Christ," the church awaits the coming of the bridegroom, ever faithful and watchful.

   - "'. . . For the wedding of the Lamb has come, and his _____ has made herself ready. Fine linen, bright and clean, was given to her to wear.' (Fine linen stands for the righteous acts of the saints)" (Revelation 19:7, 8).

   - Our fellowship empowers our worshipful expectancy, courageous witness, and worthy walk as we await the coming of Jesus.

What a privilege to be part of His church, His "called-out ones," His body, His temple, His bride! Take a moment and give thanks to Him for this wondrous blessing of our connection with Him and with each other!

Lord Jesus,

Thank You for placing us into Your body, the church. Thank You for connecting us through the Holy Spirit with Yourself and with each other. I want to participate as a fully functioning member of Christ's body, using my gifts, talents, and skills for Your glory and for the building up of Your body. Enable me to cooperate with You fully in Your work of conforming me to the image of Christ as I seek to walk by the power of Your Spirit in the light of Your people.

In Your name, Amen.

177

Life Application

Others-Centered Love

"'. . . The Father loves the Son and shows him all he does . . .'" (John 5:20).
"'. . . I have obeyed my Father's commands and remain in his love . . .'" (15:10).

God's love is characteristically focused on others. Even the Father "focuses" on loving the Son and the Son "focuses" on loving the Father. To have received this love at your new birth is to have partaken of the divine nature through the renewing work of the Holy Spirit.

This divine "others-centered" nature is birthed in us as we yield to the Holy Spirit in order that we might love as Jesus loved.

Consider some of the ways in which Jesus loved those around Him:

- He loved Zacchaeus by accepting him, looking beyond his faults to his needs (Luke 19:1–10).

- He loved the little children with affection, touch, and affirming words (Matthew 19:13–15).

- He loved Mary in her pain with tear-filled eyes of comfort (John 11:35).

- He loved Peter in his failure with promises of prayer and restoration (Luke 22:31, 32).

Just before He went to the cross, Christ gave a new command: that we love one another as He loves us (John 13:34, 35).

Prayerfully reflect on the people in your life as you ask for the Father's "revealing" concerning others-centered love. Pause to consider which of them might benefit from God's acceptance or affection, care or comfort, prayer or promised restoration.

Which of the mentioned "others-centered" dimensions of Christ's love could . . .

- your spouse most benefit from? *My spouse could benefit from* _____
_____ .

- your children most benefit from? *My children could benefit from* _____
_____ .

- your work associates most benefit from? _____ *could benefit from*
_____ .

- a friend most benefit from? _____ *could benefit from*
_____ .

Meditate on John 20:21: "'. . . As the Father has sent me, I am sending you.'" Listen in your spirit for Jesus sending you to minister love to specific people in your life.

Scripture Memory

1 John 4:12

"No one has ever seen God; but if we love one another, God lives in us and his love is made complete in us."

Chapter 7

Transformed Character

"Therefore I, the prisoner of the Lord, implore you to walk in a manner worthy of the calling with which you have been called" (Ephesians 4:1 NASB).

One of my favorite Bible verses early in my Christian life was 1 Timothy 4:8 (NASB): "For bodily discipline is only of little profit, but godliness is profitable for all things. . . ." I would often apply this verse (very inappropriately) to rationalize my avoidance of physical exercise. Teresa's discipline in regards to health and nutrition has always been commendable, while mine has been greatly lacking. When her example and encouragement bothered me, I would respond with a flippant, "You take care of physical exercise—I'll take care of the spiritual." I avoided bodily exercise because I did not want to make the required changes in my lifestyle, which I was certain would be painful, inconvenient, and difficult.

Walking in a manner worthy of our calling requires that we exercise ourselves unto godliness (v. 7 KJV). We must spiritually train ourselves to hear and yield as God reveals Himself through His Son, His Word, and His people:

- Fresh encounters with Christ through prayer, meditation, and worship will become frequent.

- We will long to spend time in the Word, allowing the Spirit to plant its truths deep within us before we seek to teach and admonish others (Colossians 3:16).

> **This walk in the light of God's Son, His Word, and His saints not only keeps us from darkness (John 12:35), but also perfects in us the likeness of Christ. Through every relationship in our lives, every situation, triumph, and tragedy, the Spirit is at work to conform us to the likeness of Christ.**

- Fellowship with God's people will become a priority as the Spirit reveals Himself through loving brothers and sisters in Christ who are partnering together to fulfill their Great Commission purpose.

This walk in the light of God's Son, His Word, and His saints not only keeps us from being overtaken by darkness (John 12:35), but also transforms us into the image of Jesus. Through every relationship, situation, triumph, and tragedy in our lives, the Spirit is at work to conform us to the likeness of Christ.

A story is told of Michelangelo unveiling a beautiful sculpture that depicted angelic glory. When asked how he could capture such splendor and divine mystery in his work, the artist responded simply, "From the block of common and flawed marble, I chip away everything that doesn't look like an angel!" It is this very work that the Spirit does in us, as we encounter divine reality in God's Word, embrace life-changing intimacy with His Son, and experience the wonder of His love through His saints. Everything in us that does not look like Christ is chipped away—such is the mystery of spiritual transformation.

An Experience With God's People

"I will give you thanks in the great assembly; among throngs of people I will praise you" (Psalm 35:18).

Pause to reflect on your own walk in God's light. Consider how you have "exercised yourself unto godliness" during your journey through this course.

- Have you been challenged to practice disciplines such as solitude, submission, or meditation in order to draw closer to Him?

- What strength or consolation have you received as the Spirit has brought fresh encounters with God's Word, His Son, and His saints?

- Has your longing to encounter God through His Son, His Word, and His saints increased and deepened?

Complete these sentences concerning your experiences of "walking in the light."

- *God's Word has "come alive" to me, particularly* (share a specific Scripture passage and what it has meant to you) _____.

(For example: *God's Word has "come alive" to me, particularly Isaiah 30:18, which has reassured me that God longs to show me grace. I have been encouraged to confess my failures to God without hesitation or fear, knowing that, because of His grace, I will find forgiveness.*)

- *I have freshly encountered God's Son, Jesus, by* _____.

(For example: *I have freshly encountered God's Son, Jesus, by picturing Him praying for me, especially during a time when I was feeling very lonely.*)

- *I have seen God expressed through other followers of Jesus as they* _____
_____.

(For example: *I have seen God expressed through other followers of Jesus as they have been willing to spend time listening to me without trying to "fix me."*)

Share your testimonies of praise with your partner or small group. Rejoice together in how God is changing you through these encounters!

TRANSFORMED CHARACTER RESTORES GOD'S PLAN.

"So it is written: 'The first man Adam became a living being'; the last Adam, a life-giving spirit. . . . And just as we have borne the likeness of the earthly man, so shall we bear the likeness of the man from heaven" (1 Corinthians 15:45, 49).

God's original design for our character was rejected by Adam and Eve in the Garden of Eden. As descendants of Adam, we bore his likeness, a likeness that had become a distortion of God's image. But as we walk in God's light, we are transformed into the likeness of "the last Adam," Jesus Christ. In the remainder of this chapter, we will explore three aspects of Christlikeness—humility, faith, and gratitude—each of which is essential to the Father's divine plan for restoring what was lost in the Fall.

God's Original Plan for Humankind

"Then God said, 'Let us make man in our image, in our likeness, and let them rule. . . .' So God created man in his own image, in the image of God he created him; male and female he created them" (Genesis 1:26, 27).

Adam and Eve were fashioned by God in His own image, making them unique among all created things. God's plan for humankind was that they might accurately reflect His character and express His glory throughout creation. To understand more fully how this plan was to be lived out, let us consider Adam's relationship with God before sin entered the world.

Man Originally Expressed Humble Dependence.
Adam was totally dependent upon His Creator. He undoubtedly was aware that, as a human, he had certain needs—food, water, air—and Adam found that every time he experienced a need, God would supply. God even took the initiative to address Adam's fundamental need for human relationship, declaring, "'. . . It is not good for the man to be alone . . .'" (Genesis 2:18). Thus, it seems that the inclination of Adam's heart in the beginning was to humbly look to God for provision in all areas of his life.

Man Originally Exercised Expectant Faith.
Imagine talking to Adam immediately after God had told him that it was not good to be alone. The conversation might have gone something like this:

"Adam, how are you doing?"
"Not good."
"What's wrong, Adam?"
"I'm alone."
"But Adam, what does that mean?"
"I don't really know, but it's not good."
"Adam, how do you know it's not good?"
"Because God said so!"

Paul states that "'. . . faith comes from hearing the message, and the message is heard through the word of Christ" (Romans 10:17). In his original state, Adam's heart was inclined to trust God and exercise expectant faith because he heard God's voice. When God revealed His plan to create a suitable helper for him, Adam, by faith, underwent God's "surgery."

Man Originally Exhibited Grateful Contentment.
After God created Eve, we get a glimpse of Adam's grateful reaction: "'This is now bone of my bones, and flesh of my flesh; she shall be called "woman," for she was taken out of man'" (Genesis 2:23). God personally blessed the new couple, encouraged them to be fruitful, and gave them authority and dominion over all other creatures (1:28–30). It seems that Adam and

Eve originally lived in complete contentment and in harmony with God and His creation. Surely they experienced abundant gratitude for God's blessings!

God's Desire to Restore What His People Lost in the Fall

What did the "first Adam" lose through sin that the "second Adam," Jesus, desires to restore by His Spirit through you and me?

As a result of the Fall, all descendants of Adam enter the world with a corrupt nature. Adam and Eve's sin brought sin to all mankind: "Therefore . . . sin entered the world through one man, and death through sin, and in this way death came to all men, because all sinned" (Romans 5:12). After the Fall,

> **We must recapture the characteristics that originally defined the relationship between God and humanity: humble dependence, which acknowledges our need for God's caring provision; expectant faith, which declares our confidence in His trustworthiness; and abundant gratitude, which gives witness to His bountiful blessings.**

inclinations and passions that were once directed toward God were directed away from and even against Him. Thoughts that were once pure and God-focused became wicked and unsettled. Willful obedience gave way to blatant rebellion. Humankind thus became hindered in carrying out its ultimate purpose: expressing the presence and glory of God.

The remainder of the Old Testament chronicles the painful results of the Fall, but it is also filled with promises and prophecies of a coming restoration. Through the birth, death, and resurrection of Jesus Christ, these promises found their fulfillment, ushering in the hope that the Creator's initial and ultimate purpose for His created might be effectively carried out.

As children of God and co-heirs with Christ (8:17), we have again been entrusted with the task of extending God's presence. But in order to fulfill this calling, we must recapture the characteristics which originally defined the relationship between God and humanity: **humble dependence,** that acknowledges our need for God's caring provision; **expectant faith,** which declares our confidence in His trustworthiness; and **abundant gratitude,** which gives witness to His bountiful blessings. This restoration of humility, faith, and gratitude will serve as the platform for our witness to God's glory.

HUMILITY RESTORED

At the Fall, humble dependence was abandoned: "When the woman saw that the fruit of the tree was good for food and pleasing to the eye, and also desirable for gaining wisdom, she took some and ate it . . ." (Genesis 3:6). In one of the saddest moments in human history, Eve, who was created to receive all she needed from the hand of her loving and gracious Creator, **took** the fruit and ate it.

Never before had Adam or Eve **taken.** They had trusted God to address their inherent neediness as humans, and had freely received His provision. But because of Satan's temptation, Adam and Eve selfishly and greedily **took** for the first time. Tragically, they discovered that taking the fruit did not fulfill their longings. Indeed, it led only to shame, guilt, fear, and an eagerness to dodge blame for their actions.

Nevertheless, the damage was done: humans ceased being grateful recipients and became takers. But selfish taking can never truly satisfy our God-created neediness. The cry of the human heart since the Fall has consistently been, "It's not enough!" It is God's desire to send us as ambassadors to this world full of self-focused, dissatisfied people in order that we might give witness to His loving care and provision through renewed humility.

Humility Is Expressed Through Dependence.

Imagine that you are one of the 12 disciples. You have left everything to follow Jesus, entrusting your life and future to this carpenter from Nazareth. Your hopes are riding on an unclear vision of His plans for a "kingdom." It is becoming increasingly clear that your Jewish leaders are not big fans of His—in fact, they are trying to kill Him, and maybe you, too!

Now imagine your reaction as you hear Jesus say, "'I tell you the truth, the Son can do nothing by himself . . .'" (John 5:19). Are you surprised by this declaration of humble dependence? Surely this One whom you are following has some kind of plan, right? Doesn't He enjoy some sense of security about the future? Are you a bit shocked when you hear Him say, in essence, "I just wait around for the Father to show Me what to do"?

Jesus' words, startling though they may be, provide the blueprint for our lives. We are called to express humility through complete dependence upon God. Faithful, maturing disciples who walk intimately with the Spirit are able to declare, as Christ did, "'By myself I can do nothing . . .'" (v. 30).

Pause and Reflect

"'. . . We do not know what to do, but our eyes are upon you'" (2 Chronicles 20:12).

Has there ever been a time when you, like King Jehoshaphat, were surrounded by obstacles? Can you remember an occasion when, not knowing what to do or where to go, you turned your eyes toward Him? Maybe it was a time when you . . .

- needed provision.

- suffered a tragic loss.

- faced great uncertainty about the future.

- needed clear direction.

- felt helpless.

Perhaps you are even going through a time like this right now.

Complete whichever of the two following sentences is most appropriate for you at this time:

I remember when _____ ,
and I was completely dependent on God.

(For example: *I remember when I was laid off from my job. I could not find work for six months, and I was completely dependent on God*).

Right now, I need to depend completely on God concerning _____
_____ .

(For example: *Right now, I need to depend completely on God concerning my oldest child. He is very sick, but the doctors cannot seem to determine what the illness is.*)

Humility Is Displayed Through Vulnerability.

A second way in which we are to demonstrate humility is by being honest and transparent regarding our hearts and our pain. Jesus modeled this kind of vulnerability as He expressed His compassion (Matthew 9:36), shared His sorrow (26:38), and wept openly for His friends (John 11:35).

In addition, we must demonstrate vulnerability concerning our faults and sins, confessing them both to God and to one another (1 John 1:9; James 5:16). The appropriate and prayerful sharing of our failures with our spouses, friends, prayer partners, or small groups helps to bring all things into the light of God's truth and grace. Such openness produces accountability before God and others, allowing us to "walk worthy" in a wicked and perverse world (Ephesians 4:1 KJV).

Similarly, each time we approach God's Word, we should first lay our lives vulnerably before the Lord, yielding to His Spirit and allowing His Word to dwell deep within us (Colossians 3:16). Then, as we teach and admonish others, we should vulnerably disclose what God has revealed to us and done in us as we have encountered Him in His Word. Every sermon, lesson, small group meeting, or one-to-one conversation should include our vulnerable testimony to the Holy Spirit's gracious, patient, and fresh work in us.

Humility Is Expressed Through Approachability.

Jesus demonstrated approachability to outcasts and sinners (Luke 7:36–50), lepers (17:11–19), the demon-possessed (Mark 5:1–20), children (Matthew 19:13–15), and commoners (9:20–22). He never used His perfect knowledge, His miraculous power, or His ever-increasing ministry responsibilities as excuses for distancing Himself from others. Faithful followers of Christ will likewise guard themselves against arrogance, aloofness, and the trappings of "big-time ministry" that so often rob us of humble approachability.

An Experience With God's Word

"Your attitude should be the same as that of Christ Jesus" (Philippians 2:5).

Ask the Lord how He would like to develop more humility in you. Then complete the following sentences:

- *I need to be more **dependent** on the Lord concerning* _____ .

   (For example: *I need to be more **dependent** on the Lord concerning my important business decisions. I tend to decide quickly on a course of action without ever asking God for His direction.*)

- *I need to be more **open** and **vulnerable** with* _____ *about* _____ .

   (For example: *I need to be more **open** and **vulnerable** with my mentor about my struggles with my temper. I need to share this weakness and ask for prayer for greater self-control.*)

- *I need to be more **approachable** (less distant, resistant, defensive, and arrogant), particularly with* _____ , *especially when* _____ _____ .

   (For example: *I need to be more **approachable**, particularly with my kids, especially when they are arguing with me about how late they should be able to stay out. I need to listen more closely to them and be more open to what they are trying to say.*)

Take turns sharing your responses with your partner or small group, and then pray for each other, asking that each person's attitude of humility might be the same as Christ's.

FAITH RESTORED

". . . The life I live in the body, I live by faith in the Son of God . . ." (Galatians 2:20).

At the Fall, Satan undermined expectant faith: "'You will not surely die,' the serpent said to the woman" (Genesis 3:4). Adam and Eve's faith was attacked as God's truth was questioned. Faith comes through hearing and accepting God's Word (Romans 10:17), and it is threatened when His Word is devalued, ignored, or denied.

Prior to the Fall, God's provision of air, food, water, and relationships (to name just a few of His blessings) simply served as a reminder to Adam and Eve that God was the appropriate object of their faith, and that they should keep their eyes and hearts fixed on Him. But when Eve gave heed to the serpent and questioned the truth of what God had said, her faith (and Adam's, in turn) was weakened. The restoration of expectant faith to the lives of His people has been on God's heart ever since.

Faith in the Old Testament

Beginning almost immediately after the Fall, the Father began to nurture the damaged faith of His children. Though Adam and Eve's descendants never experienced the perfect faith that their ancestors had originally enjoyed in the Garden, many of them nonetheless brought pleasure to their Creator by demonstrating a measure of faith. It was by faith that Abel offered a sacrifice pleasing to God, Enoch walked with God, Noah built the ark, and Abraham followed God toward an unknown destination (Hebrews 11:4–8). Throughout the Old Testament, obedient followers of God exhibited faith in the face of difficult circumstances.

> **Throughout the Old Testament, faithful followers of God brought pleasure to their Creator by demonstrating faith in the face of difficult circumstances.**

Of course, the Old Testament is also full of instances in which people failed to demonstrate faith in God's provision: Sarah laughed at God's promise of a son (Genesis 18:10–12); the children of Israel feared that God would let them die in the wilderness (Exodus 14:10–12); the ten spies insisted that they could not possess the land of Canaan (Numbers 13:26–33); and Jonah ran from the Lord rather than trusting His instructions (Jonah 1:1–3). In order for humankind to experience more mature faith, they would first have to encounter One who modeled perfect faith.

Faith in the New Testament

Jesus, the "second Adam," lived out the perfect faith that the first Adam lost. As recounted in the Gospels, Christ consistently demonstrated confidence in God's power and provision. One clear example of the Son's faith in the Father is found in the account of the resurrection of Lazarus (John 11:1–44). After assuring Mary and Martha that their brother would live again, Jesus paused in the midst of the crowd and publicly thanked God for the miracle of Lazarus' resurrection, before it had even occurred (vv. 41, 42)! Expectant faith in the Father was a constant theme in Christ's life, ministry, and miracles. Even as he drew His last breath, Jesus demonstrated faith by committing His spirit to the Father's care (Luke 23:46).

The perfect faith that Jesus modeled inspired His followers to exercise expectant faith as well. Following the ascension and the coming of the Holy Spirit, the disciples' faith, which had been tried greatly following the crucifixion, continued to grow and strengthen, and they soon began to perform miracles of healing and deliverance just as Jesus had. The remainder of the New Testament bears witness to the power of the faith that comes through knowing Christ.

Faith Among God's Children Today

The journey toward restored faith that began following the Fall continues in the present day. Like the children of Israel and the New Testament disciples, we, too, often struggle to resolve the tension between our desire to live faith-filled lives and our tendency as fallen humans to doubt God's provision.

Often in my own life, I have faced this struggle. One of the ways in which God has spurred me on toward greater faith is through the example of my children.

When my son, Eric, was a youngster, his favorite attire was a "Spiderman" shirt. Having to part with it, even for a routine wash, was traumatic. So when our washing machine broke down beyond repair, Eric was understandably concerned about being separated from his shirt indefinitely. After he had bombarded me with questions like, "Why can't I wear it dirty?" and "When will the washing machine be fixed?" I responded with what I hoped would be sufficient explanation: "We don't have the money to fix it right now. When we get our tax refund in the mail, we'll get a new one."

Rather than dwelling on his frustration, Eric exercised great faith. When it was his turn to pray at dinner, he blurted out, "Thanks, God, for sending the tax check Saturday so we can buy a washer and wash my Spiderman shirt. Amen."

Teresa and I were speechless. We hoped that maybe he would forget what he had prayed before Saturday arrived. After all, though God is all-powerful, cooperation by the IRS was also needed here! But Eric did not forget, and repeated the same prayer at every meal that week.

Saturday came. Eric woke early, dressed, and waited for the postman. After running out to meet him, Eric returned excitedly to his speechless parents with the only piece of mail that had come that day—the IRS check!

The unflinching, childlike faith that Eric exhibited is the kind of faith that God desires to birth in all of His children, no matter their age. This is what He has been working toward since the moment of Adam and Eve's sin. Let us now consider the characteristics of the genuine faith that God is seeking to restore in His followers.

Characteristics of Genuine Faith

Faith Is Expectant.
Faithful followers of God fully expect Him to "show up." They remain mindful of the ways in which He has provided and intervened in the past, being careful to ". . . forget none of His benefits . . ." (Psalm 103:2 NASB). Faith-filled disciples declare what **can** happen, what God **can** do, rather than focusing on all the reasons why things will not work out.

Faith Is Unshakeable.
Genuine faith is undergirded by a firm confidence in the Father's love. Mature disciples of Christ follow His leading until they can no longer clearly see the path ahead of them, at which point genuine faith prompts and empowers them to take the next step. Anxiety, worry, and fear give way to the peace that passes understanding (Philippians 4:7). Upon what foundation does such unshakeable faith rest? Upon the simple truth that the heavenly Father knows what we need (Matthew 6:32). Since He knows, and we know that He cares, we can be at peace, believing in faith that He will guide and protect us.

Faith Is Sacrificial.
In stark contrast to the first Adam's selfish taking, the last Adam willingly laid down His life for others, believing, by faith, that the Father would bring forth unimaginable good through His sacrifice. So it is with faith-filled followers of Jesus. Confident that their heavenly Father is thinking of and caring for them, maturing disciples are free to think of and care for others. The temptation to fearfully take is replaced by the desire to graciously give, and the self-centered life gives way to one in which the Holy Spirit often whispers, "It's not about you—it's about Him!"

Pause and Reflect

"Now faith is being sure of what we hope for and certain of what we do not see. This is what the ancients were commended for" (Hebrews 11:1, 2).

Recall again Christ's gathering with His followers in the upper room. It is only hours before His betrayal, torment, and death. Soon, He will "become sin" at Calvary.

But notice . . .

- His **expectant** faith: "Jesus, knowing that the Father had given all things into His hands, and that He had come forth from God and was going back to God" (John 13:3 NASB).

Notice where His focus is **not:** He is not focused on self, circumstances, or what He does not have.

Notice where His focus **is:** on His Father and on what the Father has given Him and promised Him.

How might your own focus need to change in order to encourage the development of mature faith?

It will be important for my focus to move from _____ *to* _____
_____ *as the Spirit reminds me of* _____
_____ .

(For example: *It will be important for my focus to move from what I wish I had—such as more money or a better job—to gratefulness for all God has provided as the Spirit reminds me of God's total faithfulness to meet all my needs.*)

- His **unshakeable** faith: He displays no anxiety about the circumstance He finds Himself in, no fears concerning the future, no worries about what others might do.

What anxieties or worries might you need to be freed from as you experience the Spirit's refining work of faith in you?

I need the Spirit to deepen my faith so that I might be freed from anxiety and worry concerning _____

_____

_____.

(For example: *I need the Spirit to deepen my faith so that I might be freed from anxiety and worry concerning how we are going to make ends meet once the baby is born.*)

- His **sacrificial** faith: "[Jesus] got up from supper, and laid aside His garments; and taking a towel, He girded Himself. Then He poured water into the basin, and began to wash the disciples' feet and to wipe them with the towel with which He was girded" (John 13:4, 5 NASB).

In the final hours of His earthly life, as Jewish leaders plot His death, Jesus Christ, being well aware of His true identity, calling, and destiny, focuses on those nearest Him. He takes on the role of the lowest servant and washes their feet.

What sacrifices might others need from you? Who might you be able to serve as you grow in mature faith?

As my confidence in God's care and provision grows, I will be freed to sacrificially serve _____ *by* _____

_____.

(For example: *As my confidence in God's care and provision grows, I will be freed to sacrificially serve my roommates by helping to clean our place; my husband by saving money on our grocery spending; my wife by taking the kids for a few hours to give her a break.*)

After sharing your responses with your partner or small group, pray together a prayer of faith, claiming the simple but profound promise that "'. . . Your heavenly Father knows . . .'" (Matthew 6:32).

As you pray . . .

- trust that He knows.
- trust that He cares.
- trust that because He cares, you need not be anxious.
- trust that, as you ask according to His will, He hears, and that you will have what you request (John 14:14).

GRATITUDE RESTORED

"For Christ's love compels us . . ." (2 Corinthians 5:14).

Concerning the tree that was in the middle of the Garden of Eden, God told Adam, "'You must not eat from the tree of the knowledge of good and evil, for when you eat of it you will surely die'" (Genesis 2:17). Satan, seizing on this command, launched a sly, cunning attack that was aimed at undermining Adam and Eve's gratitude toward God.

Notice the subtlety of the serpent's approach: He began by simply asking Eve, "'Did God really say, "You must not eat from any tree in the garden?"' Eve replied, "'We may eat fruit from the trees in the garden, but God did say, "You must not eat fruit from the tree that is in the middle of the garden, and you must not touch it, or you will die."' Satan immediately retorted, "'You will not surely die . . . when you eat of it your eyes will be opened, and you will be like God'" (3:1–3).

Notice how Satan's words implied that Adam and Eve had "needs" beyond those things that Jehovah Jireh had committed to provide. It is as if he was saying, "Eve, you need to be able to eat from **all** the trees—you need to be like God. What kind of God would not let you eat from any tree in the Garden? What kind of God would put a tree there and then say 'Don't eat from it'?"

For the first time, Eve's focus shifted from all the abundance that was hers to the one thing that was forbidden. By shifting her focus from what she had to what was prohibited, Satan was able to convince her to embrace lies concerning God's character, leading her to believe that her Creator was stingy and unnecessarily restrictive rather than generous and full of grace. Abandoning their gratitude, Adam and Eve selfishly took from the fruit of the tree, and, true to God's word, they died—instantly in spirit, and eventually in body as well.

The Transforming Power of Gratitude

In our day, have we not been subjected to this same subtle attack? Does gratefulness for the infinite love of Christ empower us, or have we bought into the lie that we have needs for which God is not committed to provide?

What is it that prompts our witness, encourages our service, and enlists our commitment? Is it merely a sense of our duty to live up to others' expectations? Is it a sense of obligation, a feeling that we must somehow "pay God back" in some measure for the forgiveness and love we have received?

May it never be! The maturing disciple's heart will be prompted often by the Holy Spirit to consider anew the wonder of being loved by God, the privilege of co-laboring with the Creator, and the awesome truth that we get to relate intimately with Christ.

> **The maturing disciple's heart will be prompted often by the Holy Spirit to consider anew the wonder of being loved by God, the privilege of co-laboring with the Creator, and the awesome truth that we get to relate intimately with Christ.**

This ever-deepening gratitude prompts faithful disciples to . . .

- remember and give thanks for all the benefits and blessings of God (Psalm 103:2).

- frequently enter His gates with thanksgiving and His courts with praise (Psalm 100:4).

- have inexpressible joy, even in the midst of a world filled with difficulties and pain (1 Peter 1:8).

- endure all things, just as Christ did at Calvary (Hebrews 12:2, 3).

- ". . . Be strong in the Lord and in his mighty power" (Ephesians 6:10).

- guard their hearts and minds against Satan's subtle lies with the peace that results from prayer and petition with thanksgiving (Philippians 4:6, 7).

An Experience With God's Son

"Therefore, since we are receiving a kingdom that cannot be shaken, let us be thankful, and so worship God acceptably with reverence and awe" (Hebrews 12:28).

Read Luke 7:36–50, the story of Jesus' encounter with a Pharisee and a sinful woman. Consider again the importance of the Spirit's restoration to us of humility, faith, and gratitude, and reflect on how each of these three characteristics is demonstrated in this story. Then read and meditate on the following story:

It was a bad idea from the start. What made her think that she could slip into the room unnoticed? The people shuffled away from her. Their hateful glares made her cheeks blaze behind her veil. No matter how hard she tried to blend in, it seemed that her very presence provoked the worst in every crowd. The furtive whispers and muffled laughter stoked the embers of her anger to a white-hot rage. Did they think she was stupid? Did they think she did not know that the jokes were about her?

Simon, the host for this gathering, was the most important Pharisee in the village. Ceremoniously, he followed the visiting Teacher into the room, quickly scanning around to make sure that all was in order. His eyes quickly locked on the woman—what was **she** doing here?

For an intense moment, she endured his glare. All ears strained in expectation of Simon's disgusted apology to his honored guest. The woman felt trapped, exposed. There was nothing to do but wait for Simon and his visitor to condemn her presence and her lifestyle. Her beating heart pounded as she stared at the floor. But no rebuke came.

Then she noticed the Teacher. *Why is He walking toward me?* she thought. Then she saw the look in His eyes. *He knows who I am!* she realized. *He knows what I have done! Why would He dare come near me? Why doesn't He act like the others?* As the Teacher smiled at her, she suddenly realized that, for the first time since she was a little girl, she had met a Man who saw her as she wanted to be and not as she had become.

The woman began to cry. *I have been forgiven*, she thought. She sank to her knees as tears poured from her eyes, seemingly washing away decades of sin and hurt. Her tears fell on the dusty, calloused feet of the Teacher.

The crowd fell silent; only her sobbing could be heard. Those in the room waited to see Simon's reaction. This Jesus was reported to be a prophet. But if He was, surely He would not allow Himself to be approached so familiarly by a common prostitute!

But Jesus did not move. His eyes ran with tears, also. Then the most amazing thing took place: Unashamedly, the woman removed her veil. Her dark hair cascaded onto the feet of Jesus, and she began to wash His dusty feet with tears and wipe them with her hair.

Her pocket held a small vial of perfume. She opened it, filling the air with a sweet aroma, and anointed the feet of the Teacher. Simon was filled with indignation. The Teacher's silence seemed to indicate His acceptance of the woman in spite of her sin. The flustered Pharisee demanded an explanation.

Jesus replied, "Simon, do you see this woman? I came into your house as a guest, but you provided no water to wash My feet. But she has washed My feet with her tears and dried them with her hair. You gave Me no oil for My head, but she has put perfume on My feet. You gave Me no kiss of welcome, but she has not stopped covering My feet with kisses. That is why I tell you, Simon, that her sins, many as they are, are forgiven, for she has so much love. But the man who has little to be forgiven has only a little love to give."

Christ's love compelled this woman to weep, to worship, to minister, to witness. It produced in her deep humility, faith, and gratitude. How about you? Have you had similar encounters with Him?

Lord, as I reflect on Your acceptance, forgiveness, and love of me, my heart is moved with _____. *I am prompted to* _____
_____.

Share your responses with your partner or small group. Then pray for one another, asking that you each might respond to the infinite love of Jesus with humility, faith, and gratitude.

CHAPTER 7 FOLLOW-UP PROJECTS
1. **Bible Study:** The Departure of the Glory
2. **Life Application:** Perfecting Holiness in the Fear of the Lord
3. **Scripture Memory:** Galatians 2:20

Bible Study

The Departure of the Glory

God's glory is at the very heart of who He is. "It is the essence of His nature, the weight of His importance, the radiance of His splendor, the demonstration of His power, and the atmosphere of His presence. God's glory is the expression of His goodness and all His other intrinsic, eternal qualities."* When God displays His glory, He is visibly demonstrating His presence among His people, and giving evidence of His desire to dwell with them.

As we have previously seen, God initially displayed His glory to the children of Israel in the cloud by day and the fire by night as He led them out of Egypt. He also made His presence known at Mt. Sinai through the spectacular sights and sounds of fire, smoke, thunder, lightning, and an earthquake. When the tabernacle was completed and the priests were fully consecrated, God again manifested Himself to His people, and His glory continued to dwell in the tabernacle until the occasion of the completion of the temple in Jerusalem. As soon as King Solomon finished his dedicatory prayer over the temple, ". . . fire came down from heaven and consumed the burnt offering and the sacrifices, and the glory of the LORD filled the temple. The priests could not enter the temple of the Lord because the glory of the LORD filled it" (2 Chronicles 7:1, 2).

Tragically, the glory of the Lord did not remain among His people indefinitely. In this brief Bible study of select passages in Ezekiel, we will look more closely at the circumstances of the departure of the glory of God from the temple. As we consider this crucial event in the history of the children of Israel, we might ask ourselves, "What was happening in the heart of God? Why would He remove His glory, the visible demonstration of His presence with His people?"

HISTORICAL BACKGROUND

During the latter part of King Solomon's reign, Israel began to fall into sin. In so doing, God's people disrespected His glorious presence among them. The people soon fell into discord, and the nation was divided into northern and southern kingdoms. As the period of the kings progressed, the people of both kingdoms fell into immorality and idolatry while their enemies

*Rick Warren, *The Purpose Driven Life* (Grand Rapids, MI: Zondervan, 2002), p. 53.

multiplied and prospered, and eventually both kingdoms were overthrown, and their people taken into captivity. The people then cried out to God, "Why have You allowed this to happen to us?" In essence, God's people accused Him of treating them poorly—of failing to fulfill His promises.

God raised up prophets to help answer the question, "Why?" One of those prophets was named Ezekiel. God gave Ezekiel incredible visions of His glory, but He also let him see what the priests and other leaders of Israel were doing, and how the heart of God was being affected.

Read Ezekiel 1 (the whole chapter, especially vv. 4–18, 25–28; see also Revelation 4).
How would you describe Ezekiel's vision of the glory of God?

_____

_____

_____

_____

Read Ezekiel 3:12, 13, 22, 23.
Ezekiel hears the sounds of God's glory, and then God's glory appears to him on the plain. How do these two encounters with the glory of God impact Ezekiel?

_____

_____

_____

_____

Read Ezekiel 8.
God's glory is again revealed to Ezekiel, this time in the inner court of the temple. But what else does God show to Ezekiel?

_____

_____

_____

Why do you think what Ezekiel sees is so significant? Why do you think God would reveal these terrible sins to Ezekiel and have the prophet record them for all of us?

_____

_____

_____

Read Ezekiel 9:3; 10:4.
God's glory appears again to Ezekiel, moving from the inner court to the threshold of the temple before stopping.

Read Ezekiel 10:18, 19.
God's glory moves from the threshold of the temple to the east gate, then stops again.

Read Ezekiel 11:22, 23.
God's glory leaves the temple, moving from the east gate out of Jerusalem to the mountain east of the city. This is the last mention in the Old Testament of the presence of God's glory among His people, Israel. The glory has departed. But **why** did it depart?

Ezekiel essentially tells the leaders of Judah who are in exile in Babylon, "God gave me a vision. He showed me all the detestable ways that you have fallen into idolatry and immorality, worshipping the pagan gods of your neighbors, rejecting and despising the true God. I saw the glory of God come up out of the temple, and I saw it leave the temple and the city. It is gone. The reason God left you is because your sinful idolatry and immorality declared to Him that you do not care whether He is with you or not. You have driven the presence of God from His sanctuary." (See Ezekiel 8:5, 6, 18; 9:9, 10; 11:1–15.)

During this period of history, Israel spurned her calling—to be God's own people among whom His glory dwelled. She lost the opportunity and blessing of expressing the presence of His glory.

Pause and Reflect

Notice that God's glory—the visible manifestation of His presence with Israel—seems reluctant to leave. The glory moves away from the inner court, then stops. It moves from the threshold of the temple and stops again. It moves to the east gate and halts once more. Finally, it leaves the temple and the city of Jerusalem completely, moving out to the Mount of Olives.

How does it make you feel to realize that God's glory was driven out of His sanctuary by Israel's terrible sin, yet it lingered? It is as if God did not want to leave. Could it be that He was hoping that someone among the leaders of Israel would notice His departure and care enough to do something about it?

What do you feel for Him? Complete the following sentence:

I feel _____ for God because _____
_____
_____.

(For example: *I feel sad for God because His own chosen people cared so little for Him that not only did they drive Him off, but that they seemed to not care at all. I feel heartbroken because He seemed to want to stay, in spite of their terrible sins against Him.*)

Take a moment now to express these feelings to the Lord. Pray, telling Him about what you just wrote. Then thank Him for the amazing privilege of being the dwelling place of His glory now!

Life Application

Perfecting Holiness in the Fear of God
(The Dread of Displeasing Him)

"Therefore, having these promises, beloved, let us cleanse ourselves from all defilement of flesh and spirit, perfecting holiness in the fear of God" (2 Corinthians 7:1 NASB).

". . . Continue to work out your salvation with fear and trembling" (Philippians 2:12).

Imagine yourself for a moment in the days of your "first love," perhaps during your teen years or young adulthood. Recall your first case of "puppy love" or, if you are married, think back to the early days of being madly in love with your spouse.

If you can remember such a time, you might recall having a dread of displeasing the one you were in love with—at all costs, you wanted to please that person. Maybe you had to have just the right outfit, haircut, or manners. Maybe you paid the price of inconvenience, exerting great effort just to be with this person in order to please him or her. On a human level, you had a "healthy" fear of letting him or her down.

"THE FEAR OF THE LORD" REDEFINED

With this backdrop of an admittedly human analogy, let us reconsider our understanding of what it means to possess the "fear of the Lord," which "is the beginning of wisdom" (Proverbs 9:10). This "fear" is not just an anxious concern that we will suffer dreadful consequences for our disobedience. That is a very childlike understanding of the situation. Out of love, parents prescribe "consequences" for wrong behavior, and children comply in order to avoid the consequences. But as maturity comes, children begin to internalize their parents' loving concern so that compliance comes to be motivated by trusting love for the parents.

So it is to be with Christ's disciples. A dread of painful consequences may motivate short-term compliance with rules and standards, but it will not motivate our whole-hearted participation in the journey toward Christlikeness. Scripture addresses the limitation of this "dread of consequences" as the aging apostle John states, "There is no fear in love," and then declares, "because fear has to do with punishment. The one who fears is not made perfect in love" (1 John 4:18).

Would God, who graced us with His infinite, unmerited, loving favor when He saved us, now seek to motivate our walk with Him through fear of consequences? Would not such fear simply cause us to seek to perfect by works that which was begun by grace, thus undermining the wonder of our worth as joint heirs with Christ and replacing it with performance-based worth?

The yielding love of the Son toward the Father, which we have received through the Holy Spirit, produces not this sort of bondage to fear, but an intimate relationship based on a genuine desire to bring God pleasure—a relationship in which "the fear of the Lord" is a deep longing to not let Him down. Faithful disciples experience wonder at having received the grace to please God and dread any word, action, attitude, motive, or initiative that might displease Him.

Pause and Reflect

Reflect back on the time when you first entered into a relationship with Jesus. Do you recall wanting to please your newfound Savior? Was a longing to avoid displeasing Him part of your new birth experience? Did you experience the desire to . . .

- "put away" certain things, attitudes, or behaviors?
- avoid certain familiar patterns and places?
- flee certain activities and acquaintances?

Complete these sentences:

As I think back on my experience of accepting Christ as my Savior, I recall these thoughts of wanting to please Jesus: _____
_____
_____.

I now desire to please Him, and dread displeasing Him. As a result, I sense a deeper motivation to yield to Him in these ways: _____
_____
_____.

Close this time of reflection by praying the following in your own words:

Dear Lord,

Thank You so much for Your infinite, personal, gracious, accepting love for me, which You demonstrated by suffering and dying on the cross for me. May I be motivated to love You and yield to all You reveal to me—not by fear of any potential consequences, but by the desire to please You and the fear of displeasing You because I love You so much.

In Your name, Amen.

Scripture Memory

Galatians 2:20

"I have been crucified with Christ and I no longer live, but Christ lives in me. The life I live in the body, I live by faith in the Son of God, who loved me and gave himself for me."

Chapter 8

Transformed Relationships

"Though you have not seen him, you love him; and even though you do not see him now, you believe in him and are filled with an inexpressible and glorious joy" (1 Peter 1:8).

It was Passion Week. After almost a year, the opposition of the Jewish religious leaders to Jesus was about to come to a climax. Throughout the week, Jesus spent time at the temple during the day and returned to Bethany at night. Perhaps He stayed in the home of His beloved friends Martha, Mary, and Lazarus. What a contrast He must have experienced: ever-increasing hostility in the daylight hours, and caring companionship at night.

During His trips into Jerusalem, Jesus had several heated debates with the religious authorities. First, the chief priests, scribes, and elders came asking, "'By what authority are you doing these things?'" (Mark 11:28). Then it was the Pharisees and the Herodians: "'. . . Is it right to pay taxes to Caesar or not?'" (12:14). Finally, the Sadducees, who did not believe there was a resurrection, came up with a scenario of seven brothers who married the same woman in turn. They then asked, "'At the resurrection whose wife will she be . . .'" (v. 23). Each time, Jesus sent His challengers away amazed, astonished, and confounded.

One day, a lone scribe stepped into this "stump the teacher" atmosphere. Scribes taught the law and were experts in it. This particular scribe had heard the debates, and had seen how well Jesus had answered the religious leaders. During a lull in the action, he posed a question to Jesus: "'Of all the commandments, which is the most important?'" (v. 28).

What was this scribe's motivation for asking? Was he, like the others, simply trying to trap the teacher in His words? Did he just love theological debate? Or did he sincerely want to know the answer? Regardless, his question was a

> **This particular scribe had heard the debates, and had seen how well Jesus had answered the religious leaders. During a lull in the action, he posed a question to Jesus: "Of all the commandments, which is the most important?"**

good one because there were so many laws to consider and obey. Jewish rabbis identified 613 individual statutes of the law and constantly tried to differentiate which were most important and which were not as important.

"'The most important one," answered Jesus, 'is this: "Hear, O Israel, the Lord our God, the Lord is one. Love the Lord your God with all your heart and with all your soul and with all your mind and with all your strength." The second is this: "Love your neighbor as yourself." There is no commandment greater than these'" (vv. 29–31).

This sobering imperative has come to be known as the Great Commandment, and it parallels and informs Christ's challenging post-resurrection directive, the Great Commission: "'Therefore go and make disciples of all nations, baptizing them in the name of the Father and of the Son and of the Holy Spirit, and teaching them to obey everything I have commanded you . . .'" (Matthew 28:19, 20). These two exhortations provide the blueprint for our transformed lives as faithful disciples of Jesus.

OUR DESTINY: LIVING OUT THE GREAT COMMANDMENT AND THE GREAT COMMISSION

As followers of Christ, we all, like Abraham, have embarked on a journey without knowing much about our destination. But consider for a moment that, together, the Great Commandment and the Great Commission might capture God's ultimate destiny for each of us. God has given us 66 books of Scripture, each of which is filled with helpful instructions and guidance for our lives, but perhaps His deepest desire is that we might truly orient our hearts, minds, and souls around just these few verses. The fulfillment of the Great Commandment and the Great Commission is the objective toward which God's transforming work in our lives is directed.

Along the journey, we must receive nourishment in order to be sustained and to grow strong. This nourishment comes as we walk in the light of God's Son, His Word, and His people. As we seek to genuinely follow Jesus, the yearning in our hearts to hear Him is so deep and passionate that we put away from our lives every sin, hindrance, and obstacle that would get in the way. Our spirits long for Him to reveal Himself in our times of worship,

> **God has given us 66 books of Scripture, each of which is filled with helpful instructions and guidance for our lives, but perhaps His deepest desire is that we might truly orient our hearts, minds, and souls around just these few verses.**

prayer, meditation, Bible study, and fellowship. As light is to our eyes, so is His revelation to our spirits. Without it, darkness will overtake us.

In addition, we must yield to that which God reveals even before we fully understand it. Christ declared to His disciples that He had "'. . . food to eat that you know nothing about'" (John 4:32). Like Jesus, our food must increasingly be "'. . . to do the will of him who sent [us] and to finish his work'" (v. 34).

The end result toward which the Spirit's transforming work is leading us is that we might live out "the simplicity and purity of devotion to Christ" (2 Corinthians 11:3 NASB) by embracing a Great Commandment identity of love and pursuing a lifestyle of Great Commission passion. It is only this identity and lifestyle that will enable us to fully and completely express the glory of God that dwells in us.

Is Transformation Optional?

I can still remember the first time in my Christian life when it occurred to me that, "I am being transformed into the image of Christ—whether I like it or not!" Led and empowered by His Spirit, I was on the journey of sanctification, heading toward the divine objective of Christlikeness.

But what if I did not want to make such a journey? What if I did not really desire to be like Jesus? In a gentle but clear way, the Spirit answered, "Tough! Just like a newborn baby has been designed to grow up into a mature human being, your spiritual new birth has set you on the course of growing into the fullness of Christ. You may hinder or temporarily side-track your spiritual growth just as you can your physical growth—through poor diet, little exercise, and unwise choices—but you are being conformed to the character of Christ."

> **Once I embraced the reality that the process of spiritual transformation was not optional, the next issue was my attitude: Would I make this journey reluctantly or indifferently, or with eagerness and initiative?**

Once I embraced the reality that the process of spiritual transformation was not optional, the next issue was my attitude: Would I make this journey reluctantly or indifferently, or with eagerness and initiative? Would I resist the Lord's work in my life and, like Saul of Tarsus, continue to "'. . . kick against the goads'" (Acts 26:14), or would I cooperate with the Lord's agenda and say, like Mary, "'I am the Lord's servant. . . . May it be to me as you have said'" (Luke 1:38)?

Even though I knew what my attitude should be, it was not until I explored an even more fundamental issue that I finally and joyfully embraced the process of transformation.

Why Our Christlikeness Is So Important to God

The deeper question for me was this: Why was it so important to God that I be transformed into the image of His Son? Was it because He wanted to control me? Was it simply a matter of "shaping me up" for heaven? I was not sure I wanted any part of God's plan of transformation until I understood His motives better.

Over time, I began to see that one reason why our spiritual transformation process is so important to God is that it enables us to live out the Great Commandment and the Great Commission. Unless we become like Jesus, we cannot really love God or love others as we love ourselves. Furthermore, until we experience this genuine, passionate love for God and others, we will not be empowered to pursue a lifestyle of Great Commission witness. It thus became clear to me that the benefits of being transformed into the image and character of Jesus are not just realized when we get to heaven. There are abundant blessings to be enjoyed and shared with others during our earthly journey as well.

I discovered three ways in which the transformation process brings blessings here and now:

1. Becoming Christlike **blesses me** as it frees me to experience the abundant life that He has promised (John 10:10 NASB).

2. Becoming Christlike **blesses others** as they experience the living letter of my life (2 Corinthians 3:3) and receive the love of God through me.

3. Becoming Christlike **blesses God,** bringing Him pleasure as I fulfill the purpose for which I have been created: "For you created everything, and it is for your pleasure that they exist and were created" (Revelation 4:11 NLT).

My heart was stirred with gratitude to God for such a wonderful plan. Slowly, my resistance and "goad-kicking" gave way to gratefulness for His love. Being transformed into the image of Christ now seemed to be not a dreaded necessity, but a blessed opportunity.

An Experience With God's Word

"'. . . He who offers a sacrifice of thanksgiving honors Me . . .'" (Psalm 50:23 NASB).

Pause to consider that God's ultimate purpose for your life—transforming you into the likeness of Christ so that you can express His glory . . .

- allows you to receive of God's abundant blessings.

- enables you to bless others with His love.

- blesses God and brings Him pleasure.

What do these truths do to your heart? Might you be touched to offer a sacrifice of thanksgiving to God, confident that such an offering honors and glorifies Him?

Share with Him your response to the following:

Jesus, as I consider the wonder that Your transforming purpose in my life actually blesses You and others around me, and that Your calling on my life also serves as one of the avenues through which You bless and provide for me, my heart is filled with _____ _____.

(For example: *My heart is filled with praise, awe, wonder, gratitude, love, joy. I cannot get over how much You love me, and I hope I never do!*)

Pause to pray with your partner or small group, giving God honor through your praise and thanksgiving.

IT'S ALL ABOUT LOVING RELATIONSHIPS!

God not only commands us to love Him and others, He also gives us the love we need in order to fulfill these commands. "We love because he first loved us" (1 John 4:19). Such truth reminds us that God's calling on our lives is not primarily related to what we believe or how we behave, but to how we love. It is loving relationships with God and people that informs biblical-centered belief and empowers righteous behavior.

The Great Commandment gives focus to loving relationships with God, others, and ourselves:

- "Love the Lord your God. . . ."

- "Love your neighbor. . . ."

- ". . . As [you love] yourself."

Our calling to join Christ in Great Commission living also requires that we give priority to relationships as we follow the Holy Spirit's leading to make disciples of others, confident that He is always with us.

The Dangers of Failing to Pursue Loving Relationships

Missing the priority of loving relationships will lead us astray from our sincere and pure devotion to Christ (2 Corinthians 11:3), and into darkness:

- The darkness of **prideful arrogance,** which leads us to become "puffed up" by how much we know or how "correct" our beliefs are compared to the beliefs of others.

- The darkness of **judgmentalism,** which entices us to consider how outwardly "righteous" we are in comparison to others.

- The darkness of **irrelevance,** which tempts us to focus on our own activity, achievements, or accomplishments, mistakenly believing that such things bring fulfillment or transformation.

Darkness began to overtake the disciples in their final hours with Christ. Several of them argued about which of them was the greatest (Luke 22:24). Peter asserted that his commitment to Jesus was superior to that of the others (Matthew 26:33). Thomas was preoccupied with which way to go, while Philip wanted to know and see more (John 14:5, 8). Imagine the scene—Jesus' closest friends have missed their calling, their purpose. Their confusion stems not necessarily from improper theology or unrighteous behavior, but from a failure to properly prioritize their relationships with Jesus and with one another. Only by steadily pursuing and improving these relationships can we avoid falling into the same darkness.

LOVING THE LORD OUR GOD

Loving Jesus Requires That We Know Him.
In order to truly love the Lord with all our heart, soul, mind, and strength, we must first know Him. Though the disciples had been with Jesus day and night for three years, their behavior during Christ's final hours on earth seemed to call into question whether they really knew Him (John 14:9).

As faithful followers of Jesus, we must be sure to grasp several key aspects of His nature.

He Is God.
Jesus consistently demonstrated His divinity—not only by His miraculous acts, but also by His words. For example, during that last night with His disciples, Jesus said, "'A new command I give you: Love one another. As I have loved you, so you must love one another'" (13:34). The fact that He referred to these words as a "command" was revolutionary. Jewish leaders would have issued laws, rituals, and rules, but never "commands." To claim the power to issue commands was to claim to be God! The Jewish authorities had Jesus put to death primarily because they refused to believe what He consistently tried to demonstrate, through word and deed—that He was and is God. As true disciples of Christ, we must recognize and acknowledge His deity.

> **As disciples of Christ, we must be ever-conscious of His abiding presence. He is always with us, always available, always approachable.**

He Is Here.
As disciples of Christ, we must be ever-conscious of His abiding presence. He is always with us, always available, always approachable. "'. . . And surely I am with you always, to the very end of the age'" (Matthew 28:20); "'Never will I leave you; never will I forsake you'" (Hebrews 13:5). Recognizing Jesus' nearness empowers us to know Him more deeply and love Him more fully.

He Has All Power and Authority.
Christ has been given all power and authority (Matthew 28:18). We can take confidence, courage, and hope from the truth that nothing is too difficult for Him (Genesis 18:14). He gives wisdom for every decision (Proverbs 2:6; James 1:5). He provides a way of escape from every temptation (1 Corinthians 10:13). No thought, attitude, or word escapes His notice.

The Apostle Paul's Passion to Know Jesus
Our calling as disciples is first and foremost about knowing God intimately, lovingly relating to Him with all of our heart, soul, mind, and strength (Mark 12:30). A desire to know the Lord in this way gripped the life of the apostle Paul, who declared, ". . . I consider everything a loss compared to the surpassing greatness of knowing Christ Jesus my Lord. . . . I want to know Christ and the power of his resurrection and the fellowship of sharing in his sufferings . . ." (Philippians 3:8, 10). These words provide several insights into the nature and importance of truly knowing God.

"I Want to Know Christ"
Paul's desire to intimately know the Lord far exceeded any other priority in his life. As faithful disciples, we must pursue this same deep knowledge of Christ if we hope to experience true transformation. Only after nurturing our spirits through communion with Him will we be adequately prepared to meet the challenges of each day and the demands of every relationship.

Practically, this life of intimately knowing Christ involves . . .

- listening for His voice during quiet times of reflection (Psalm 46:10; Matthew 17:5).

- spending time praising His works, as well as worshiping Him simply because of who He is.

- emulating His dependence on the Father in our own times of prayer and meditation.

- focusing on the Gospels' illustrations of His compassion, thus gaining insight into how He desires to live through us.

"The Power of His Resurrection"

Paul goes on to express his desire to experience the new life and power that were made available to all believers through Christ's sacrifice and resurrection. The apostle describes this power further in Ephesians 1:19, 20, where he prays that we would all know ". . . his incomparably great power for us who believe. That power is like the working of his mighty strength, which he exerted in Christ when he raised him from the dead. . . ." Jesus' death and resurrection empowered His followers to come to know Him more deeply by several means:

- Because Christ died and rose, we can live **in union with Him,** drawing on His strength, wisdom, and love: ". . . I no longer live, but Christ lives in me . . ." (Galatians 2:20).

- Because Christ died and rose, we can live **for Him,** dedicating ourselves to the pursuit of His will and the advancement of His kingdom: "And he died for all, that those who live should no longer live for themselves but for him who died for them and was raised again" (2 Corinthians 5:15).

- Because Christ died and rose, we can live **as His representatives,** extending His presence into the world by the power of His Spirit: "We are therefore Christ's ambassadors, as though God were making his appeal through us . . ." (2 Corinthians 5:20).

- Because Christ died and rose, we can live **to glorify Him,** responding with gratefulness and wonder to the grace given to us: ". . . you are not your own; you were bought at a price. Therefore honor God with your body" (1 Corinthians 6:19, 20).

"The Fellowship of Sharing in His Sufferings"

Christ was indeed who He claimed to be—the last Adam, the Word become flesh. He was fully God, yet fully human. In his humanity, He identified with us. He was tempted in all ways, acquainted with sorrow, despised, and rejected. He understands us. In exploring the depths of His suffering, we find the reassurance that we are not alone, and receive the hope to carry on.

- Christ understands our struggles, trials, and pain: "He was despised and forsaken of men, a man of sorrows and acquainted with grief . . ." (Isaiah 53:3 NASB). "For we do not have a high priest who is unable to sympathize with our weaknesses . . ." (Hebrews 4:15).

- Christ identifies with our loneliness and distress: "'My soul is overwhelmed with sorrow to the point of death . . .'" (Matthew 26:38).

- Christ comprehends our pain; we are not judged or condemned for it: ". . . The Lord longs to be gracious to you; he rises to show you compassion . . ." (Isaiah 30:18).

An Experience With God's People

". . . If we ask anything according to his will, he hears us. And if we know that he hears us—whatever we ask—we know that we have what we asked of him" (1 John 5:14, 15).

We know that Christ is with us—yet our homes, workplaces, communities, choices, words, thoughts, and attitudes often show little evidence of His presence. Consider Jesus' sad words to His disciples: "'Have I been so long with you, and yet you have not come to know Me?'" (John 14:9 NASB). He might very well ask the same of us. He is desperate for us to see Him as He really is—not inspecting, disappointed, or distant, but excited to love us. He longs for us to know Him as the apostle Paul sought to—intimately, powerfully, lovingly.

Consider your own life: In what areas do you need to experience more of His presence? Be still before the Lord, inviting Him to speak.

Complete the following sentence, circling or underlining any answers that apply to you:

Lord Jesus, I sense that I need to encounter You, acknowledge You, and depend on You more . . .

- *in my relationships with family members and friends.*

- *in my workplace or community.*

- *in my thoughts and attitudes.*

- *in my words.*

- *in my emotions.*

- *in my choices.*

- *in prayer, solitude, and meditation.*

- *in worship and Bible study.*

- *in my witness and lifestyle.*

- Other: _____.

Share your responses with the Lord. He is already here with you, available, approachable. Tell Him of your desire to acknowledge Him, listen to Him, and yield to Him.

(For example: *Lord Jesus, I sense that I need to depend on You more in my financial choices. I tend to make decisions without really praying for Your guidance. Perhaps that's why some of my decisions have turned out to be pretty bad.*)

Now share your responses with your partner or small group. Then take turns praying for one another, claiming the promises of 1 John 5:14, 15: that God hears you, and that He will bring about the things for which you have prayed together.

LOVING OURSELVES

Loving Ourselves Requires Embracing Our True Identity as the Beloved of God.

"'. . . As I have loved you, so you must love one another'" (John 13:34).

With these words, Jesus is both reminding the disciples of His past demonstrations of love and concern for them, as well as foreshadowing His forthcoming display of perfect love at Calvary. Through His sacrifice, and through His continual caring involvement in our lives, Jesus has loved us as well. The more that we recognize and receive His love, the more we are able to embrace our true identity as His beloved.

Consider what Scripture reveals about God's love for us:

- God demonstrated His love for us by sending Jesus to die for us while we were still sinners (Romans 5:8).

- Nothing can separate us from God's love (Romans 8:38, 39).

- He has poured out His love upon us through the Holy Spirit (Romans 5:5).

- The love of Christ for us is infinitely great and surpasses knowledge (Ephesians 3:18, 19).

- Because of His great love for us, God made us alive with Christ (Ephesians 2:4, 5).

We are not simply people who believe Scripture's great doctrines about Christ, nor are we merely people who practice good behavior. Hopefully, we **do** believe right doctrine and practice right behavior, but we must be careful not to think that our identity lies in either of these things.

> **Our true identity is that we are ones who have been loved by Jesus.**

Our true identity is that we are ones who have been loved by Jesus. Genuine discipleship requires imparting the wonder of this truth to men, women, youth, and children, thus helping them to see themselves as God sees them.

The Challenge of Embracing our True Identity

Our journey toward genuine discipleship begins with the simple realization that we are the recipients of divine love, the beloved of God. That is our identity. But embracing this identity is far from automatic. Many Christians faithfully attend church, read their Bibles, and give of their finances without ever really experiencing the reality of God's love for them. They may attend countless seminars, work through several discipleship curricula, and read dozens of books on the spiritual life, yet they remain painfully unaware of their identity as God's beloved.

Satan often attempts to deceive us into believing that our identity is solely based on what we do, thus causing us to focus on how we have failed or where we have fallen short, and to question whether God could really love us in the face of such shortcomings. If we buy into this lie, we will never have great boldness and passion for what we have been called to do. All the evil one has to do to hinder our effectiveness in embodying the Great Commandment and fulfilling the Great Commission is to prevent us from recognizing our true identity.

> **Satan often attempts to deceive us into believing that our identity is solely based on what we do. . . . If we buy into this lie, we will never have great boldness and passion for what we have been called to do.**

Embracing Our True Identity: A Testimony

When my wife, Teresa, speaks in our ministry conferences, she often shares a story from the early days of our relationship, which is relevant to the issue of identity. As you read her account, allow the Holy Spirit to quietly remind you of who you are.

"I don't know if they still do this today, but when we were in high school, the thing to do was to somehow be identified with your boyfriend. Maybe you would wear his big class ring, or you might wear his letter jacket. Somehow, this communicated that, 'I belong to somebody.'

"When David and I were dating, I took this idea of 'identifying with him' one step further. Instead of wearing the class ring or the letter jacket, my girlfriend and I decided one day that we would get out on her roof in our swimsuits, and we taped our boyfriends' initials on our backs. We then laid out in the sun for a few hours.

"After we were done with our sun bath, we took the tape off. We then had our boyfriends' initials on our backs. My identity was now imprinted on my flesh. I was the girlfriend of D.L.F.—David L. Ferguson.

"Many years later, I was reading through my Bible and God spoke to me about my identity. I was reading Isaiah 49:15, 16, which says, 'Can a mother forget the baby at her breast and have no compassion on the child she has borne? Though she may forget, I will not forget you! See, I have engraved [or tattooed] you on the palms of my hands.' I sensed God saying to me, 'Teresa, you know something about those initials on your back? In time they faded. Eventually they could have even been replaced by somebody else's initials. But you are indelibly, permanently tattooed on the palms of My hands. You belong to Me. You are identified as Mine.'

"We are His beloved—we have been impressed indelibly on His heart."

Experiencing Being God's Beloved: The Startling Love of Jesus

Perhaps you are wondering how, in the midst of countless competing priorities and battles with self, Satan, and the world, we can possibly embrace and live out our identity as God's beloved. Not many days go by without my heart needing to be led by the Spirit back to the wonder of this truth. During times of solitude, or drives from the airport to out-of-town meetings, I often meditate in the hopes of having fresh encounters with the "startling love" of Jesus.

Christ's words were startling and His miracles amazing, but everything He said and did was meant to call attention to how He loved. Take a moment now to reflect on how Jesus loved people and how He startled them with His love.

Jesus startled lepers by healing their bodies and bringing dignity to their lives, sometimes even touching them in order to heal them (Luke 5:12, 13; 17:11–19).

> **Christ's words were startling and His miracles amazing, but everything He said and did was meant to call attention to how He loved.**

Christ startled a Samaritan woman when He broke all cultural conventions by asking her for a drink of water. In the midst of her shame and rejection, the Savior entrusted her with a conversation about eternal things (John 4:4–26).

Jesus startled the woman caught in adultery when He knelt down beside her, joining her at the point of her hurt and providing protection for her life. He dispersed her accusers with His words, and then offered restoration to her as He lovingly said, "'Woman, where are they? Has no one condemned you? . . . Neither do I condemn you. Go now and leave your life of sin'" (8:10, 11).

Even at Calvary, in His final hours, Christ startled people with His love:

- Imagine how He must have startled those Roman soldiers—the very ones who had mocked Him, tortured Him, driven the nails into His hands and feet, and gambled for His clothing—as He looked at them and said, "'Father, forgive them, for they do not know what they are doing'" (Luke 23:34).

- Consider the thief who was crucified next to Christ. After a lifetime of deception, he must have been startled to hear Jesus' accepting words: "'. . . Today you will be with me in paradise'" (v. 43).

- Recall Jesus looking down from the cross and seeing His mother, Mary, standing with His beloved disciple, John. Once again, Christ displayed His startling, supportive love. Looking ahead to His approaching death, He made provision for His mother, saying to her, "'Dear woman, here is your son,'" and to John, "'Here is your mother.'" The Bible says that from that day forward, Mary lived in the house of John (John 19:26, 27).

Picture Jesus in agony on the cross. He is prepared to take upon Himself the sins of the world. He will soon sense that His own Father has turned His back on Him, and will cry out, in a voice that conveys a feeling of utter abandonment: "'My God, my God, why have you forsaken me?'" (Mark 15:34). Yet there He hangs, still startling people with His love. He is dying, yet He is thinking of those around Him. He is giving up His life, yet He is still giving life to others so that they might know His love. That is the startling love of Christ.

> **He is dying, yet He is thinking of those around Him. He is giving up His life, yet He is still giving life to others so that they might know His love. That is the startling love of Christ.**

For whom did Christ do all this? For whom did He suffer and die? Listen as the Spirit whispers, "He did it for you! If He did not need to die for anyone else, He would have done it just for you!" Allow this wondrous truth to motivate you to walk in the light of His love.

LOVING OTHERS

". . . He poured water into a basin and began to wash his disciples' feet . . ." (John 13:5).

We might expect that, on the last night of His life on earth, Jesus' mind would have been filled with thoughts of His impending death. But as He and the disciples concluded their Passover meal, Christ demonstrated that His attention was not fixed on Himself, but on His friends. He took a towel and a basin and washed the disciples' feet—including even the feet of Judas, who would soon betray Him for 30 pieces of silver.

The Gospel of John tells us that this humble act of service was motivated by Jesus' knowledge ". . . that the Father had put all things under his power, and that he had come from God and was returning to God" (John 13:3). It is the same with us: The key to really loving others is knowing who we are, where we came from, and where we are going. As we embrace the wondrous truths that God loves us, that we have been forgiven and accepted, that we are being transformed into His image, and that we will one day rule and reign with Him, we are freed to genuinely serve others in love. Conversely, if we are intent on trying to prove to everyone that we are right or that we are "somebody," or on trying to exert our rights or maintain our position, we will have a hard time handling a bowl of water and a towel.

A Message to Empower Today's Church

As we live in awareness of who God really is, and embrace our identity as His beloved, we gain clarity, discernment, and empowerment, enabling us to pursue the calling of the true disciple. We are here to relate lovingly with God and with those around us, making Him known as we extend and express His glorious presence.

Hearts filled with "Great Commandment love" empowered the witness of the first century church. The accounts found in the Book of Acts make it clear that the early Christians loved God with their whole being and loved their neighbors as themselves:

"They devoted themselves to the apostles' teaching and to the fellowship, to the breaking of bread and to prayer. Everyone was filled with awe, and many wonders and miraculous signs were done by the apostles. All the believers were together and had everything in common. Selling their possessions and goods, they gave to anyone as he had need. Every day they continued to meet together in the temple courts. They broke bread in their homes and ate together with glad and sincere hearts, praising God and enjoying the favor of all the people. And the Lord added to their number daily those who were being saved" (Acts 2:42–47).

We find similar encouragement in the New Testament letters. In Romans 13:9, 10, Paul

> **Hearts filled with "Great Commandment love" empowered the witness of the first century church. The accounts found in the Book of Acts make it clear that the early Christians loved God with their whole being and loved their neighbors as themselves.**

states that every other commandment may be summed up in the rule, "Love your neighbor as yourself," and asserts that, "Love is the fulfillment of the law."

Other verses similarly focus on the importance of love:

- "Keep on loving each other as brothers" (Hebrews 13:1).

- "You, my brothers, were called to be free. But do not use your freedom to indulge the sinful nature; rather, serve one another in love" (Galatians 5:13).

- "And now these three remain: faith, hope and love. But the greatest of these is love" (1 Corinthians 13:13).

- John's burdened appeal to the church at Ephesus was, "'. . . You have forsaken your first love'" (Revelation 2:4).

In light of Matthew's end-time prediction, "Because of the increase of wickedness, the love of most will grow cold" (Matthew 24:12), the restoration of Great Commandment hearts and Great Commission lifestyles among God's people may represent both the most significant challenge and the greatest opportunity for the 21st century church.

"You Will Be My Witnesses in Jerusalem and in Judea and Samaria and to the Ends of the Earth."

We Are Here to Be Witnesses of His Life and Love to Those Nearest Us (Our "Jerusalem").

God's ultimate purpose for my life will begin at home, with my spouse, children, family members, and friends. Because of the closeness of these relationships, they provide both ongoing challenges that intensify Christ's sanctifying work, and opportunities for creating "living legacies" by imparting our faith. In this day of increasingly fragmented and unhealthy relationships, marriages, families, and single adult friendships that have Christ as their center will provide the foundation for a convincing witness of Christ's life and love.

Those who are married are called to demonstrate love toward their spouses and to commit themselves to consistent enrichment, mutual giving, and shared vision within their marriage. Parents are entrusted with a calling to pass on the faith to their children, passionately prioritizing the spiritual development of their dear "disciples." This family-focused approach contributes to the health and witness of our broader church involvement. "Being the church" in our homes prepares us to serve others well.

We Are Here to Be Witnesses of His Life and Love to Those of the Household of Faith (Our "Judea").

Caring connections within Christ's church support His plans for our maturity. Through the Holy Spirit's illumination, each member of the body comes to understand his or her gifts and callings more clearly. Mutual care and encouragement provide a place of refuge from the world's darkness. As we join together in worship, study of the Word, prayer, and communion, we experience the building up of the body.

As we engage in genuine fellowship, we come to understand God's love more clearly through our love for one another—which is sometimes demonstrated through serving and giving, sometimes through exhortation and reproof—and thus find security in our identity as His beloved. Through fellowship, we learn the relational skills of love (1 Corinthians 13), embody the compassion of Christ's heart (2 Corinthians 1:3), and come to share the Lord's burden for those who do not know Him.

We Are Here to Be Witnesses of His Life and Love to Those We Encounter in Our Daily Lives (Our "Samaria").

Jesus' parable of the Good Samaritan provides important insights regarding our Great Commandment/Great Commission calling. In response to the inquiry "Who is my neighbor?" Jesus illustrates key principles concerning our witness. In contrast to the irrelevant religion of the priest and Levite, Christ's love will . . .

- sensitize our spirits to those around us, so that we may not miss opportunities to give an account of the hope that is within us (1 Peter 3:15 NASB).

- touch our hearts with His compassion as we come to see people as He sees them—alone, hurting, and sometimes in trouble and bondage.

- empower us to go "across the road" in order to . . .

  ◆ minister His acceptance to those who have failed.

  ◆ extend His comfort to those in pain.

  ◆ share His support with those who are struggling.

We Are Here to Extend His Life and Love to the Uttermost Parts of the World, to "Go and Make Disciples of All Nations."

This global call to share Christ's likeness and love with all people is accompanied by His promise that "'. . . I am with you always . . .'" (Matthew 28:20).

As we transition from our time in this course of study to our ongoing journey of expressing God's glory as true disciples, let us close with one last time of experiencing Christ together.

An Experience With God's Son

"'Come to me, all you who are weary and burdened, and I will give you rest'" (Matthew 11:28).

Jesus invites us to come to Him in our weariness:

- Maybe you are weary of the world's ways.

- Maybe you are weary of seeking life fulfillment in what you have acquired, achieved, or accomplished.

- Maybe you are weary of competing demands and ever-changing priorities.

- Maybe you are weary of seeking to live in your own strength.

- Maybe you are weary of trying to love by your own power.

Imagine Jesus standing before you right now, gazing intently at you. His eyes are full of compassion, and if you listen closely, you will hear Him say, "'Take my yoke upon you and learn from me, for I am gentle and humble in heart, and you will find rest for your souls'" (v. 29).

Picture now in your mind Christ standing before you. Maybe He is wearing flowing robes and sandals. Perhaps He has a bearded face. Maybe your image is of the resurrected Christ, with nail-pierced hands and feet. But as you look closer, you notice that He is standing in a yoke. One side of the yoke is around His neck, while the other is empty. He extends His invitation for you to join Him, to learn from Him. Hear again the words, "Take my yoke upon you." It is your invitation to join Him, to partner with the One who is love in extending His love to others.

Listen as you hear Christ speak to you:
- "I consistently love those around you, but I often do so alone—would you come join Me?"

- (To husbands) "I support and comfort your wife, but I often do it without you— would you come join Me?"

- (To wives) "I encourage and affirm your husband, but I often do it without you— would you come join Me?"

- (To parents) "I am attentive to your children's hearts and sensitive to their innermost needs, but I am often caring for them alone—would you come join Me?"

- "I am taking initiative to lovingly sacrifice on behalf of those that you encounter in your daily life, but I often do so without you—would you come join Me?"

Now meditate on your yielded response to the Spirit's revelation of Jesus' invitation.

In your own mind and heart, picture yourself rising to join Christ in the yoke. Imagine yourself standing alongside this One who is love.

Pray now with your partner or small group, sharing with Christ your response to this blessed privilege and wondrous calling.

Lord Jesus, as I meditate on the wonder that I have been called to join You in this divine purpose, and that I can learn from You how to better love those around me, my heart is filled with _____.

I particularly sense Your call on my life to join You in loving these specific people:
_____
_____

Continue to change and conform me, that Your love and presence might be even more clearly expressed through me.

I claim Your promise that, "Faithful is He who calls you, and He also will bring it to pass" (1 Thessalonians 5:24 NASB).

About the Author

David Ferguson and his wife, Teresa, have shared a biblical message of health and relevance for more than 25 years. Their passion for seeing the Great Commandment of loving God and loving others lived out among God's people has enabled them to impact thousands of ministers and their laity. As co-directors of Intimate Life Ministries, they direct a multi-disciplinary team that serves more than 35,000 churches in the United States and abroad with training and resources through the strategic partners involved in the Great Commandment Network of denominations, movements, and ministries. David serves as co-director of the Center for Relational Leadership, which provides training and resources in church, business, and community settings.

About The Great Commandment Network

The **Great Commandment Network** is a team of denominational partners, churches, para-church ministries, and strategic ministry leaders that is committed to the development of on-going Great Commandment ministries worldwide. Great Commandment ministries help us love God and our neighbors through deepening our intimacy with God and with others in marriage, family, church, and community relationships.

The **Great Commandment Network** is served by *Intimate Life Ministries* through the following:

- **The Center for Relational Leadership (CRL)**—Their mission is to teach, train, and mentor both corporate and ministry leaders in Great Commandment principles, seeking to equip leaders with relational skills so they might lead as Jesus led. The CRL then challenges leaders to train their co-workers in these relevant, relational principles because great relational skills can and will impact customer/member satisfaction, morale, productivity, and, ultimately, an organization's measurable success.

- **The Center for Relational Care (CRC)**—Their mission is to equip churches to minister effectively to hurting people. The CRC provides therapy and support to relationships in crisis through an accelerated process of growth and healing, including Relational Care Intensives for couples, families, and singles. The CRC also offers training for counselors and caregivers through More Than Counseling seminars.

- **The Center for Relational Training (CRT)**—Through a team of accredited community trainers, the CRT helps churches establish ongoing Great Commandment ministries. They offer an online supported, structured process for guiding church leaders through relational ministry training. Training is available in a variety of relational areas: Marriage, Parenting, Single Adult Relationships, Leadership, Emotional Fitness, Care-giving, and Spiritual Formation.

- **The Galatians 6:6 Retreat Ministry**—This ministry offers a unique, two-day retreat for ministers and their spouses for personal renewal and for re-establishing and affirming ministry and family priorities. Co-sponsoring partners provide all meals and retreat accommodations as a gift to ministry leaders.

- **Great Commandment Radio**—Christian broadcasters, publishers, media, and other affiliates build cooperative relationships in order to see Great Commandment ministries multiplied.

- **Relationship Press**—This team collaborates, supports, and joins together with churches, denominational partners, and professional associates to develop, print, and produce resources that facilitate ongoing Great Commandment ministry. Experiential, user-friendly curriculum materials allow individuals, churches, and entire denominations to deepen Great Commandment love. Great Commandment Ministry Online provides tools for relationships and the workplace including helpful downloads such as family-night tips, marriage staff meeting ideas, daily couple devotionals, and ways singles can reach out to other single adults by meeting relational needs. Tools for the workplace include goal setting, time management, and life-balance assessment.

For more information on how you, your church, ministry, denomination, or movement can become part of the Great Commandment Network and take advantage of the services and resources offered by Intimate Life Ministries, write, call, or visit our website:

Intimate Life Ministries
P.O. Box 201808
Austin, TX 78720-1808
1-800-881-8008
www.GreatCommandment.net